1999

COMPETITIVE
and ETHICAL?
How **Business** Can
Strike a **Balance**

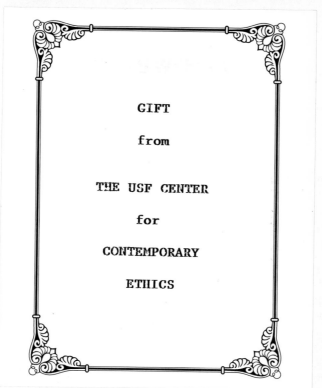

GIFT

from

THE USF CENTER

for

CONTEMPORARY

ETHICS

YOURS TO HAVE AND TO HOLD

BUT NOT TO COPY

First published in 1998

Kogan Page Limited
120 Pentonville Road
London N1 9JN

British Library Cataloguing in Publication Data

A CIP record for this book is available from the British Library.

ISBN 0 7494 2669 1

Typeset by Kogan Page
Printed and bound in Great Britain by Biddles Limited, Guildford and King's Lynn

Contents

List of acronyms

The increased use of acronyms counts among the unattractive features of the second half of the twentieth century, but they do have their uses provided that insiders do not employ them to shut out the uninitiated in any discussion of human affairs. They can also be a barrier between nations: some anglophones have problems with the French ONU and OTAN – until they spell them backwards, that is.

Below is a list of most of the acronyms used in this book. Apologies to those to whom they are obvious: British readers may be mildly resentful of the fact that CBI has to be explained as the Confederation of British Industry, but in the US it stands for the Caribbean Basin Initiative and in India the Central Bureau of Investigation.

AA	Advertising Association (UK) *	GNP	Gross national product
ABC	Audit Bureau of Circulations (UK)	HSBC	Hong Kong Shanghai Bank
ACCA	Chartered Association of Certified		Corporation
	Accountants (UK)	IBE	Institute of Business Ethics
AGM	Annual General Meeting		(UK) *
ASA	Advertising Standards Authority	IBM	International Business Machines
	(UK)	ICC	International Chamber of
ASB	Accounting Standards Board		Commerce *
	(UK) *	ICI	Imperial Chemical Industries
BA	British Airways	IGO	Intergovernmental Organization
BBC	British Broadcasting Corporation	IMF	International Monetary Fund
BCCI	Bank of Credit and Commerce	IoD	Institute of Directors (UK) *
	International	J&J	Johnson and Johnson
BG	British Gas	JL	John Lewis Partnership
BitC	Business in the Community	KLM	Royal Dutch Airlines
	(UK) *	M&S	Marks & Spencer
BOC	British Oxygen Company	MD	Managing Director
BP	British Petroleum	MP	Member of Parliament (UK)
BT	British Telecommunications	NAPF	National Association of Pension
CAP	Common Agricultural Policy (EU)		Funds (UK)
CBI	Confederation of British	NBA	Net book agreement (UK)
	Industry *	NGO	Non governmental organization
CD	Compact disc	OECD	Organization for Economic
CEFIC	European Federation of Chemical		Co-operation and Development
	Industries	OFT	Office of Fair Trading (UK)
CEO	Chief Executive Officer	PC	Personal Computer
CFCs	Chlorofluorocarbons	R&D	Research and Development
CoE	Council of Europe	RSA	Royal Society of Arts (UK) *
EAT	European Advertising Tripartite	RTZ	Rio Tinto Zinc (now Rio Tinto)
EBRD	European Bank for Reconstruction	SCF	Save the Children
	and Development	SME	Small or medium-sized company
EU	European Union	TI	Transparency International *
FCPA	Foreign Corrupt Practices Act (US)	UK	United Kingdom
FIDIC	International Federation of	UNCED	United Nations Conference on
	Consulting Engineers		Environment and Development
FSA	Financial Services Authority (UK)	UNICEF	United Nations Children's Fund
FTC	Federal Trade Commission (US)	US	United States of America
GATT	General Agreement on Tariffs and	WBCSD	World Business Council for
	Trade		Sustainable Development
GCC	Global Climate Coalition (US)	WTO	World Trade Organization
GM	General Motors	WWF	Worldwide Fund for Nature

*See Appendix G for details

Foreword

by Tim Melville-Ross
Director General, Institute of Directors

People in business know that their work is absolutely central to society. They also recognize that the wealth-creation process is essential to provide the revenues to pay for all those public services that people need, and not least those they care about most – healthcare and education. Many members of the public do not understand this adequately and have a distrust of business, which is only too easily fuelled by widely reported scandals.

Competition between businesses is equally essential, so that consumers can get the best value from the goods and services they buy. In competing hard with one another, businesses need to show that, however tough the going may be, they conduct themselves with integrity and show due respect not only for their investors but also for their employees, customers, suppliers, the environment and society at large.

I believe that this is why business has to create its own vision, both in terms of its purpose and the values that it holds dear, and that it must communicate this much more clearly than it has done so far to the rest of society. Business people need to bring their positive contribution to the attention of the public as never before, but they can only succeed in doing so if they themselves conduct their businesses in a morally acceptable manner.

Much of the valuable writing on these topics comes from people who do not have a business background and do not know at first hand just how hard it is to compete successfully without cutting moral corners. This book is an exception, having been written by someone who has spent all his life in industry and commerce and who has drawn widely from the experiences of many others. It is easy to read, thought-provoking and controversial. There will be few readers who will agree with everything in it, myself included, but that is in the nature of the subject.

The book is intended to stimulate ideas and offer support and advice to people at all levels in business who would like to go about their work with integrity, however tough the competition may be. It should also be a help to students of business who are about to start careers in manufacturing, trading or service industries.

I also hope it will prove to be a help and encouragement to business men and women who, by the manner in which they conduct themselves, will act as good ambassadors for the business community.

Preface

This book is a celebration of competition. As the title implies, it is aimed at helping people in business to compete hard, while going about it in an ethical manner. 'What?' asked the Swiss banker with a grin, '*Are* there any ethics in competition?' A New York businessman said he thought it would be a very short book. Indeed, these reactions are typical of many people to a book on this subject. Perhaps that is as good a reason as any for writing it.

In direct contrast to these comments, a very senior manager in a highly ethical company, who was consulted about this book, wrote: 'Its subject matter is very much at the forefront of sensible business thinking at the moment.' Indeed, it is intended to pose controversial questions that are central to business and its place in society. It is especially appropriate as we take stock of such issues in the run-up to the millennium and beyond.

The attitude to business on the part of many sections of society in Britain is still far more negative than in many other countries that are our commercial competitors. As long ago as 1986, it was (rightly) thought necessary to stage an Industry Year to try to explain the role of business in a more positive light to the British people; this was followed up with some success through the activities of the Royal Society of Arts (RSA). However, business is unfortunately still not regarded highly enough by the public. Anti-business prejudices are easily nurtured by instances of wrongdoing and moral turpitude (especially on environmental issues) to which the media properly draw attention, even if at times they blow them up out of all proportion. Furthermore, the recognition of some of the benefits arising from the application of market principles, including competition, to public services has been tempered by doubts about both their effectiveness and their morality.

The comments above may apply mainly to Britain, but they are just as relevant in other countries. Whilst many of the examples and mini case studies quoted throughout the book are based on real-life experiences in the UK, there are just as many drawn from multinational companies and businesses operating (mainly) in the rest of Europe and in North America.

Much has been written on business ethics generally by economists, sociologists, politicians, management gurus, philosophers and theologians, but less about the ethics of competition itself. In writing on this subject, it has been necessary to exercise discipline by trying to avoid straying into wider areas of business ethics, while on the other hand sticking firmly to competition in business and ignoring that of politicians for votes, teenagers for scholarships, the unemployed for jobs, or sportsmen and women for medals.

Because of the very nature of its subject, the book starts with a chapter on the economics and morals of competition. This is extended to an outline of the religious aspects of the subject in Appendix A. In Chapter 2 there is discussion of the various ways in which competition is limited, some of which are ethical and some of which are not.

However, the main purpose of the book is to offer practical guidance to business people on the difficult and complex problems they encounter in their daily struggle to compete in the marketplace. Chapters 3–5 deal with many such problems and offer advice to companies and individuals, based not on theory but on the practical day-to-day business experience of the author and many others.

It is a truism that business people of principle can be faced with serious dilemmas as practical considerations come into conflict with moral principles. Indeed, they are fortunate if they are just faced with dilemmas – choices between only two courses of action; more often than not, their task is much more complex, which critics of business only too often fail to comprehend.

This book aims in particular to support those individuals who may sometimes feel that their personal moral principles are in conflict with those of their organizations. This is particularly relevant when the company is suffering from severe competitive pressures and its employees are feeling personally insecure. At such times the company and its individual members need to overcome these pressures without taking moral short-cuts. In this respect, Chapters 6 and 7 are the heart of the book, offering advice on where help can be obtained and how action may be taken to try to avoid such situations arising.

Of course there are no simple formulas, no 'quick fixes' on how to deal with specific situations; an easily accessed textbook on such matters would be superficial in the extreme. This book is merely a tool but, it is hoped, a useful one that complements the work done by various bodies to encourage companies and business and professional organizations to develop statements of values and codes of ethical practice appropriate to their particular sphere of activity. Such codes, providing they are effectively promulgated at all levels in the company or firm, can provide individuals with much-needed guidance and support.

Just as business deserves respect from society for its contribution through wealth creation, so competition deserves to be recognized for the benefits it brings. When either falls short, that respect and recognition are diminished. It follows that, just as business itself has to behave ethically, so the achievement of competitiveness needs to have an ethical dimension.

It is absolutely vital to compete, to be a winner in business, but not at all costs. This is not just a matter of obeying the law and avoiding doing wrong in order to compete because, as is argued in a positive and practical way in Chapter 7, ethics can themselves be moulded into building blocks of competitiveness.

Acknowledgements

Behind this book lies a great deal of inspiration over many years from members of the Advisory Board and the Executive Committee of the Institute of Business Ethics, and from the work done by that body in the first twelve years of its existence. It would be invidious to mention some of the people concerned and to exclude others.

Thanks are also due to Dominick Harrod of St George's House, Windsor, for help and advice on the first chapter; Bishop John Jukes, Rabbi Pinchas Rosenstein of the Jewish Association of Business Ethics and Dr Zaki Badawi of the Muslim College, who helped in providing the Christian, Jewish and Muslim perspectives (respectively) for Appendix A; Susan Bennett and Carlota Bedwell of the Royal Society of Arts, who gave invaluable help in obtaining books and giving access to the papers on their *Tomorrow's Company* project; Simon Webley for extensive help and guidance on his work on codes; Martin Wassell and other former colleagues at the International Chamber of Commerce for bringing me up to date on their self-regulatory codes; Philip Spink of the Advertising Association for advice on Chapter 3; Derek Walker of Worldaware for allowing me to make use of reports on symposia on bribery used in Chapter 4; and Amanda Bowman of Business in the Community for help in finding positive examples in Chapter 7. Invaluable critical comments were made by Stephen Walzer on matters pertaining to competition law and on aspects of Chapter 4, and David Sarre advised on the book as a whole. There were many others, too numerous to mention, who have given me help in other ways.

One, however, deserves very special mention: my wife, Anne, whose forbearance as we competed for access to our computer and whose invaluable and expert help in error-spotting and proof-reading made the whole undertaking possible.

The views expressed are those of the author and, because the subject is by definition controversial, not everyone mentioned above will agree with it all – if they did, it would be the duller for it. Moreover, there are no easy answers to the questions discussed – otherwise there would be little need to embark on the project in the first place.

I am also grateful to the authors of the books and articles quoted in the text, most of which are listed in the bibliography at the end. This is deliberately not an academic work, so the clutter of footnotes has been avoided, but it is still hoped that people teaching business studies will find it both readable and useful to their students. They and other readers may wish to look at some of the books – many of them, by design, far from recent – that have helped me try to achieve some representation from both the enthusiastic supporters of competition and the sceptics.

Giles Wyburd

Chapter 1

The economics and morals of competition

There is much to celebrate about competition. In a market economy, it brings out the best in business and is the best possible way of ensuring benefits to customers. Yet a celebration of competition without any reservation would be a grave error. It is far from perfect and much wrong is done in its name. The central theme of this book is that business can do itself (and the very idea of competition) nothing but good by competing in an ethical manner. What matters, above all, is *how* companies compete with one another.

Charles Handy, in *The Hungry Spirit*, says that 'competition generates energy, rewards winners and punishes losers'. In that short sentence he sums up the benefits and warns of the flaws. This chapter seeks to spell out both.

SOME DEFINITIONS

What is competition in business? For the purpose of this book, it is the interaction between companies in buying and selling goods and services that establishes prices, levels of sales and, as a consequence, market share, profitability and continuity. Competition is most effective when there is substantial freedom of entry and exit for participants, where there is a large number of sellers and buyers without undue imbalance in size between them, and when those buyers are well informed about the products in question.

Competition is much more than a matter of selling a better product at the same price as a rival firm, or selling a similar product at a lower price. A company can still compete by selling a superior product at a higher price, for example a settee to last twenty years instead of ten or a health-care policy offering higher levels of benefit. Furthermore, price and quality are far from the whole

1

story. It is not only professional marketers who recognize the many other important factors that apply, including delivery, payment terms, after-sales service, availability of spare parts, professionalism of authorized distributors, the clarity of product descriptions (especially in service industries), the user-friendliness of manuals and instructions, and the quality and effectiveness of advertising and promotion.

There can be healthy competition within an industrial group consisting of highly devolved operating companies as they seek similar new markets or compete for capital investment from the parent. And competition is not necessarily restricted within a business sector: companies in widely differing businesses can compete for a share of consumers' disposable income. For example, car dealers can be pitched against greenhouse suppliers, while both can find themselves fighting for business against travel agents and companies offering pension schemes.

Competition is complicated, tough and constantly demanding. The pressures inherent in trying to succeed in it create a constant challenge to corporate and personal ethics.

What are business ethics? For the purpose of this book the answer is very simple: they provide the essential moral underpinning of how business is conducted. An ethical business operates according to moral values that permeate all its activities and guide and give support to all the people who work in it.

In essence – and this is the thrust of this book – it is not just what a company does, what products and services it sells and what they cost that count, but the perception of the integrity of the company itself and its employees, which is also enormously important. As is spelt out in detail in Chapter 7, a competitive company is one from which people want to buy, to which they want to sell, for which they want to work and in which they want to invest. Such a company will have a high reputation with its customers, its suppliers, its own employees and their immediate dependants, its shareholders and lenders, not forgetting the local communities around its sites and the public at large.

THE ECONOMIC BENEFITS OF COMPETITION

'A horse never runs so fast as when he has other horses to catch up and outpace,' wrote the poet Ovid nearly two thousand years ago. This implies that competition gets the best out of those engaged in it (it can also bring out the worst in us, but more of that later) and it also brings great benefit to others. In the words of Dominick Harrod, a former Economics Editor of the BBC, who has an extraordinary skill in explaining complicated economic matters in clear language to ordinary people, 'the economic benefits of competition are as follows:

- it is the best known means of providing choice through quality, service, variety and price

- it is one of the best ways of finding out what people want, measuring whether the demand can be met and providing the incentive to do so

- it reduces sustained excessive profits, providing market entry is not too difficult or costly for newcomers

- it ensures efficient allocation of resources

- it stimulates innovation and productivity

- it is a driving force of creativity and stimulates economic progress

- it obviates monopoly, which can so easily lead to lax behaviour and insensitivity to the needs of consumers.'

The last point in the above list typifies the production-orientated approach and lack of competition that can occur anywhere but that was particularly marked in the former Soviet bloc, where the reverse of the first six points prevailed in an economy that was inefficient in the extreme and that bore very little relation to the needs of the consumer. Indeed, many readers will have experienced the transformation of the UK telecommunications market as competition intensified in the 1990s, albeit with some extra nudges from the regulator (the role of regulators is discussed briefly in Chapter 2). The consequent improvement in services and the price reductions in real terms experienced by consumers are the envy of many other countries.

The landmark report on corporate social responsibility, produced by the Confederation of British Industry in 1973 under Lord Watkinson's presidency, was quite clear on this: 'Free competition in an open market is the consumer's best assurance of obtaining value for money.' This is as true today as it was then. The customer may indeed be the prime beneficiary of competition, but in fact weaker companies can also benefit, provided that they are able and ready to react to competitive challenges and improve their performance.

When Japanese car makers first appeared on the US and European markets, there was a lot of wailing and gnashing of teeth from domestic producers, along with demands to exclude the intruders through protectionist practices, some of which lasted far too long. There were numerous casualties, but in the end those that managed to survive did well by improving their production methods and their products to the benefit both of their customers and themselves. It would be churlish, for example, not to give some credit to Japanese competition for the spectacular improvement in the perceived quality of the vehicles produced between the 1960s and the 1980s by the General Motors subsidiaries, Opel and Vauxhall, and the same would apply to all the other survivors in the motor manufacturing business.

It is understandable that business people can be ambivalent about competition. When they are in a strong competitive position and are expanding sales and market share, they like it. When business is not so good and competitors are gaining ground on them, they only too often complain that it is unfair. Badly run businesses often blame the competition for their own shortcomings, when it is just those shortcomings that give rivals their advantage. To well run companies, competition is a necessary and valuable spur to do better.

THE FREE MARKET APPROACH

The practical benefits of competition put forward by proponents of free markets owe their origins to ideas developed 200 years ago by Adam Smith and the Utilitarians such as Jeremy Bentham. Smith's main thesis in *The Wealth of Nations* in the context of this book is that 'every individual is continually exerting himself to find out the most advantageous employment for whatever capital he can command. It is his own advantage, indeed, and not that of the society, which he has in view. But the study of his own advantage naturally, or rather necessarily, leads him to prefer that employment which is most advantage to the society.' Here we have his concept of the benign influence of the 'invisible hand', which ensures that business people, by pursuing their own advantage, thereby do the greatest good for society by advancing general prosperity.

Smith's concept of the pursuit of legitimate self-interest is necessary for the achievement of competitiveness. Indeed, one modern commentator, Stephen Green, in his book *Serving God? Serving Mammon?* published in 1996, credited Smith with bringing the phenomenon of competition to 'centre stage', establishing it in 'the market place at the centre of commercial transactions and of economic progress'.

These principles were developed further by the Utilitarians, believing as they did in the 'greatest happiness of the greatest number', and help to support the case for competition made in the preceding section of this chapter. Adam Smith and the Utilitarians would indeed see the 'invisible hand' at work in today's competition between companies for markets and profit as leading to the public good.

The view of Milton Friedman and his monetarist followers was that companies should keep to their primary purpose of serving the self-interest of shareholders, explaining that the one social responsibility of business is to use its resources and engage in activities designed to increase its profits. While this view is now considered by many to be 'old hat' and has lost ground in the last few years, most people would agree with Friedman's assertion that companies in pursuit of those profits should stay 'within the rules of the game' and engage 'in open and free competition, without deception or fraud'.

In his book *Capitalism and Freedom* Friedman stated that in the US 'anyone is free to set up an enterprise, which means that existing enterprises are not free to keep out competitors except on quality and price'. This last point is dealt with in greater depth in Chapter 2. Three themes were dominant in Friedman's thinking: profits first, and then honest dealing and the exercise of competition to exclude the power of monopolies. In 1995, twenty-three years after Friedman's book came out, Samuel Brittan wrote *Capitalism with a Human Face*, in which he defends the individualist ethic, but says it still 'allows plenty of space for altruism and fraternity', describing the market as 'an instrument of human co-operation'. Writing about the former Soviet bloc, where we have in recent years seen the emergence of the unacceptable face of capitalism in its crudest form, Brittan sets out one of the key themes of this book: 'Most thoughtful economists have always known that markets need a background not only of formal laws, but also of accepted rules of behaviour, if the invisible hand is to work.'

THE ECONOMIC AND MORAL CHALLENGE

While in many respects the views of Friedman and his followers have become widely accepted, there are still reservations about some of them.

Modern commentators, such as Will Hutton in his 1995 best-seller *The State We're In*, are not prepared to trust the market. While recognizing that it is 'capable of producing great wealth, productivity and of sponsoring innovation', he says it can also be 'unstable, irrational and quite capable of producing perverse results'. In favouring more regulation, he leans towards the views of John Maynard Keynes and his later disciples.

Keynes said little directly about competition, but his distrust of *laisser faire* stemmed from his concern about what he saw in 1924 as excessive overseas investment and his favouring of domestic investment as likely to reduce unemployment. Dominick Harrod, whose father Roy Harrod wrote one of the standard works on Keynes, sees this as a 'crucial' stage in the development of familiar Keynesian ideas. At that time, Keynes saw the economic structure as far from elastic and subject to too many strains arising from the diversion of capital investment from home to abroad. 'The old principle of *laisser faire*,' he wrote, 'was to ignore these strains and to assume that capital and labour were fluid.' Given trade union rigidity and the preference of the City of London for foreign investment, the exercise of *laisser faire* prevented the free flow of capital into domestic investment.

Dominick Harrod quotes the key passage from which came Keynes's doctrine of intervention in capitalist enterprise in order to mitigate the impact of pure competition on employment, poverty and inequality: 'We are brought to my heresy – if it is a heresy – I bring in the State; I abandon *laisser faire* – not enthusiastically, not from contempt of that good old doctrine, but because, whether we like it or not, the conditions for its success have disappeared.'

In a lecture, also in 1924, Keynes summed up his attitude as follows:

> For my part, I think that Capitalism, wisely managed, can probably be made more efficient for attaining economic ends than any alternative system yet in sight, but that in itself it is in many ways extremely objectionable. Our problem is to work out a social organization which shall be as efficient as possible without offending our notions of a satisfactory way of life.

So here we see the concept which was later dubbed as capitalism (and competition) with a human face.

Over seventy years later Will Hutton, as an admirer of Keynes's ideas, contemptuously dismissed competition in the UK as 'a public school ethic, transposed to the national economy', linking it with the way businessmen call for level playing fields, the sentiment which 'has graced a thousand after-dinner speeches at employers' organisations over the decades'. In Hutton's view, the level playing field of competition can never exist because information is distributed unfairly between the players, 'so economic efficiency may not result from competition, and the players are perfectly within their rights to play the game according to different rules'.

Readers who have actually experienced competition may well have some difficulty in going along with this reasoning. They might feel that the best comment on it is the remark of the economist Alfred Marshall, who wrote: 'Every short statement about economics is misleading (with the possible exception of the present one).' This could equally apply to many of Friedman's views, which are not acceptable either; in particular those on the limited social responsibility of business have been widely rejected, as is discussed in Chapter 7.

In celebrating competition and the benefits it brings, it is important to understand why many outsiders and some business people still have doubts about it and what those doubts are. Some caution is needed here, because competition, which is essential to successful market economies, is often blamed excessively for their imperfections, when in practice it is one of the best mechanisms for overcoming them.

A form of war

One of these concerns stems from the idea that the ultimate form of competition in human affairs is war. Discussion of the 'just war', and whether all sides are in the end losers, has no place here, but some business people see competition, at least metaphorically, in terms of war.

For example, Sir John Harvey-Jones, in his book *Making it Happen,* wrote:

> When the full force of competition hits, it is desperately hard to recover your company, set the new tempo that is required, and seize the initiative back from the competition, for, remember, at that stage he will be hitting you not only with his carefully-laid plan for the first phase of his attack, but also ... he will have his reinforcements grouping for a second or third attack.

Modern war can result in near-total destruction of the enemy; similarly, in business, competitors can be eliminated from the market. This gets to the heart of the concerns of the doubters, namely that competition is violent deep down and involves winning *and* losing, the Darwinian concept of the survival of the fittest.

Losers as well as winners

Charles Handy, in *The Empty Raincoat*, wrote that 'only one firm can be industry leader ... but there has to be more to life than winning or we should nearly all be losers'. It is generally accepted that if a company fails because its products are outdated, its marketing poor or the management of its cash flow incompetent, then it is inevitable it should go down and its customers turn to more efficient competitors.

H B Acton, in his essay on the ethics of competition published in *The Morals of Markets and other Essays*, took the view that 'In competition the failure of the losers is a consequence of the success of the winners, not something the winners aim to secure.' This shows competition as more benign than a form of war, though it is not always true, as perpetrators of predatory pricing have from time to time demonstrated. However, even if the motivation of the winner(s) is not destructive, there are still casualties. What worries moralists is not so much the failure of a company (shareholders and owners know they are risking their capital) as the damage to individual employees and the effect on the communities that depend on them.

The counter-argument is that, in reality, the effect need not be so brutal; in a modern economy, we are not in a zero-sum game, because the market can often be stimulated to expand. However, the idea that there is always enough scope and space for everybody is regarded by Sir John Harvey-Jones as optimistic.

For a long time this has been an issue as regards competition from developing countries, which raises a whole series of other questions of moral equity and also economic arguments relating to open trade and the international division of labour. These are discussed briefly under the heading of Trade Protectionism in Chapter 2.

However much economists argue that there is a natural and necessary weeding-out process that improves efficiency and brings general benefit, many sociologists and others are troubled about the consequences and the moral issues involved. Charles Handy agrees that competition is a necessary spur to increased efficiency, but says 'it is easy to lose ourselves in efficiency, to treat that efficiency as an end in itself and not a means to other ends'. Further, in an interview with the *Financial Times* in February 1996, Richard Giordano, previously Chairman of BOC and then Chairman of British Gas, said: 'I'm a believer in capitalism, but it creates casualties. It's important to look after them. If capitalists ignore this, they do so at their peril.'

Unemployment

Above all, competition is blamed for contributing to unemployment. Yet, as we all know, it is technology that has led to a massive reduction in the need for people in both manufacturing and service industries and, as is so often forgotten, for the elimination of many kinds of boring and repetitive semi-skilled or unskilled work. Some such jobs have indeed moved from the richer developed countries to the poorer developing ones, but many (including repetitive typing for instance) have gone altogether and competition cannot be blamed for that except to the extent that the technology is harnessed differently by competing companies.

In recent years people have ceased to believe – with good reason – that the redundancies of some will make the jobs of the survivors safer. This has brought even more blame on competition than on the true cause of the problem, which is structural change, itself an inevitable aspect of any dynamic and changing economy.

Whether unemployment is caused by redundancies or by companies failing altogether, it is generally accepted that the state should intervene to help the individuals involved by using taxpayers' money, much of which is generated in the first place by successful businesses.

Human failings

Another worry of the doubters is that competition, driven as it is by the self-interest of competing companies, may result in benefits to customers, but that the ends do not justify the means. As has already been said, competition can bring out the worst in people as well as the best. Thus some moralists would prefer to see a higher motivation behind competition. E F Schumacher in *Small is Beautiful*, wrote: 'The market is the institutionalisation of individualism and non-responsibility,' while Charles Handy wrote in *The Empty Raincoat*: 'The market is a mechanism for sorting the efficient from the inefficient, it is not a substitute for responsibility.' The economist Alfred Marshall is quoted by Samuel Brittan as saying that the case for competitive markets arose from the 'imperfections which still cling to human nature', which means relying on stronger motives – notably self-interest – rather than on higher ones.

Preferences for co-operation

Another reason why many moralists distrust competition is that they much prefer co-operation and greater cohesion in society generally. To them, harmony and benevolence are infinitely more preferable to aggression, rivalry and strife. This is obviously a view held strongly by the major religions, as is described further in Appendix A. Speaking of society generally, they are quite right, but this does not necessarily mean there is anything unethical about competition.

Nevertheless, there are areas where it is right for there to be co-operation in business, mainly through trade and business organizations. In arrangements of this kind, members of such organizations have to be careful to confine themselves to well-defined matters of common interest, such as joint lobbying of governments, and to avoid actions limiting, or seeming to limit, competition among themselves, which would lead to managed markets and cartels.

Distrust of the market system

Many of the doubts about competition come from those who dislike and distrust private business generally and large companies in particular – especially multinationals. It is unfortunate that for historical and social reasons this phenomenon appears to have been more widespread in the UK than in the countries that are its main competitors.

When wrestling with moral questions of any kind, the easy answers are the privilege of those at the extremes of the argument. Such people are not troubled by doubt, seeing the issues in black and white only. Red-blooded believers in the supremacy of the market and competition tend to see the doubters as either ignorant or naïve; their opponents at the other extreme feel that the free-market system excludes ethical principles altogether and see its supporters as ruthless and uncaring. Both these extremes often see those in the middle as either unprincipled, or weak and easily influenced.

The fact remains that, when any company allows itself to enter into an illegal or morally unacceptable business practice, it only has itself to blame for the consequences and immediately provides convenient confirmation of the prejudices of the critics.

Indeed in such cases it is not only the perpetrator that suffers damage: a whole business sector or even a whole business can be affected. In *Ethics in Organisations* David Murray warns against the tendency of critics to argue from the particular to the general when reporting on business scandals. 'There is a risk,' he writes, 'of exaggerating the degree to which these cases of scandal are typical of the behaviour of business as a whole.' Murray has a point: the media have much to answer for, because the bad news about business sells more newspapers than the day-in, day-out good news about companies competing ethically. Throw in a few anti-business prejudices in the minds of individual journalists and a preference for over-simplistic sensationalism, and the damage can be devastating.

There have been enough business scandals in the closing years of the twentieth century, some of them arising out of the pressures of competition, to increase distrust of business in the minds of large sections of the public. The combination of such scandals, with negative perceptions about redundancies, reduced security of employment and concern for the environment, have led to the belief on the part of too many people that too many companies just do not care enough about the community around them, let alone their own customers and employees.

Opinion surveys indicate that people who are successful in a harshly competitive environment are perceived as having the lowest level of social conscience. Even if such people are prudent enough to obey the law, they are likely to sail very close to the wind on matters that, while not illegal, are of doubtful morality.

CONCLUSION

This book is less concerned with the morality and common prudence involved in compliance with the law than with unethical practices undertaken in the name of competition and not adequately covered by the law. Whether within the reach of the law or not, such unethical practices (dealt with in Chapters 3 to 5) only do damage to the moral justification of competition and business itself which, like every other field of human activity, is always let down by its worst performers.

Moral reservations about some aspects of competition there may be, but it has to be accepted as a fact of modern life. People in business today have to deal with the situation in which they find themselves. Life 'at the coalface' is never easy or comfortable, especially for people of high principles.

Whatever may be said about it, in practical terms competition is highly beneficial to society and greatly superior to the alternatives. Some business leaders and outside commentators regard competition itself as morally neutral, and only the actions, good and bad, that are taken in its name are seen to be appropriate objects for moral scrutiny. Competition, said Sir Dermot de Trafford, is like water: everything depends on how it is used – for sustaining life or for drowning.

It is obvious that all these moral aspects of competition are based fundamentally on the doctrines of the three monotheistic religions – Christian, Jewish and Muslim. An outline of their attitudes to competition is to be found at Appendix A.

The common ground between the followers of all three religions and agnostics of high moral principle is, quite simply, *how* people at the forefront of business compete with one another. This is indeed the central theme of this book.

Chapter 2

Limits to competition

This chapter deals with some of the ethical aspects of those areas where, for one reason or another, competition is restricted or limited in some way. Government intervention through competition law could in most instances reduce or eliminate such restrictions or limits, but there are nevertheless situations where competition is impractical, inappropriate or ineffective, making it necessary to take special measures to protect the consumer. In some areas, such as public services and utilities, there is intense political and ethical debate as to whether competition and other market forces should apply at all or, if they should, to what extent they should be regulated.

Competition from foreign countries can also be severely limited by trade protectionist measures. This is a vast subject and highly technical in itself, but some of the ethical aspects of it will be discussed briefly. There is also mention of another area where competition is limited by law and which raises ethical questions, namely the protection of intellectual property. Paradoxically, there are also cases where unbridled competition, which may be favourable to the consumer in the short term, may turn out to be less desirable in the longer term. Examples of these, drawn mainly (but not exclusively) from the transport sector, are discussed at the end of this chapter.

RESTRICTIVE PRACTICES IN INDUSTRY

Adam Smith is often quoted by people who distrust business as saying: 'People of the same trade seldom meet together, even for merriment and diversion, but the conversation ends in a conspiracy against the public, or in some contrivance to raise prices.' Although few would admit it, many business people are happy to be relieved of competition from time to time. Some might say that because competition makes life uncomfortable for directors, it is quite natural they should want to reduce it through cartels, monopolies, state aids and subsidies or any other means at their disposal.

This is natural, of course, but unacceptable. Yet it has to be acknowledged that because the rewards arising from price cartels or market-sharing arrangements seem to be so great, some business people are tempted to overcome the ethical reservations that may have stood in their way. In fact, the rewards often prove to be rather less than expected, and those seeking extra reward in this way only attract more and more legislation to counter such practices.

Market dominance

Many companies aim quite legitimately to become market leaders in their particular business. Achieving such a position can indeed provide welcome relief from troublesome competition, but if too successful it can also attract the attention of legislators.

There is a false belief that some companies are dominant in the markets in which they operate just because they are very large. Old-style Marxists, and others, use the word 'monopoly' as a term of abuse against big business. Comparisons between the turnover of multinationals and the gross national product of small countries are made to support the argument that such companies wield too much power. This is intellectually dishonest because the power of such companies, which is very considerable, mainly lies in the choice of where or where not to invest; it has little to do with monopolistic market dominance.

Takeovers can alter that situation, so that competition law has to be invoked. In such instances the media and the public are often more interested in the ethics of how the takeover is achieved rather than in the extent by which competition is reduced. The competition regulators are only concerned with the realities of market dominance.

There are times when competition cannot be as open as many would like it to be. Apart from clear-cut cases of market dominance by one company, the more common phenomenon is an oligopoly – domination by a very few large companies. In some markets this is inevitable, because of the very high investments required and therefore the extreme difficulty for newcomers to enter the market.

One of the best examples of oligopoly on a world scale is the international civil airframe business, where the Europeans have had to pool their resources of development and production in Airbus, while its main world competitor is Boeing, the dominant manufacturer in the US. The $15 billion merger of the latter with McDonnell Douglas in 1997 evoked some very strong misgivings in Europe, especially in France, with allegations of conspiracy and counter-allegations of paranoia criss-crossing the Atlantic.

The European Commission's competition directorate investigated the US companies' merger for five months amid concerns about cross-subsidization from military expenditure, allegations that the essence of competition law was being compromised, and threats of a trade war. In the face of all this, an important concession was made by Boeing to agree to scrap long-term exclusive supply arrangements with three of the leading airlines of the United States. All of this made it even more urgent for the European partners in Airbus to work more closely together. This situation raised so many key questions relating to competition that few doubted it was essential for governments to intervene through their competition authorities.

There is one example from the late 1990s of market dominance, arising from superb products and astute marketing, where state intervention of some kind appeared to be inevitable. This was in an industry that is the complete opposite to airframes because the physical resources required to enter the market are minimal (apart from brainpower) – the computer software industry.

It was a source of amazement to old hands from manufacturing industry when the market capitalization of Microsoft exceeded that of General Motors and Bill Gates joined the ranks of the world's richest men. In the early stages, the obvious merits of the Windows operating systems evoked wide admiration and tremendous sales success. One of the big advantages, both for the company and its customers, was the compatibility of its systems with other users of personal computers worldwide. There was, however, no such admiration in the minds of the loyal supporters of the products of Apple computers. There had, after all, been a lawsuit that they had lost, in which it was alleged that Microsoft had adopted in Windows many of the characteristics of Apple's own operating system. When, in August 1997, these bitter rivals announced that they would be co-operating with one another in several different ways, a number of competitive questions arose. Paradoxically, the links could result in Apple, which had been losing market share for some time, being saved from extinction, which was much in Microsoft's interest if government intervention on grounds of market dominance was to be avoided. Yet at the same time the arrangements allegedly strengthened Microsoft's position vis-à-vis its rivals in the battle for control of entry into the Internet (through the 'bundling' of its Windows operating system with its Internet Explorer), so risking triggering penal intervention from the US competition authorities.

This is an example of a very young market that will develop dramatically in the first years of the new century. Because the cost of entry is not high, there will be plenty of new players, notably from developing countries such as India (not for nothing did Mr Gates announce he was setting up a research facility there). Governments themselves will find it difficult to catch up with the new issues involved and to intervene when necessary. Market dominance may therefore be hard for Microsoft to retain or for others to achieve.

There are some rather less obvious ways of dominating a market; one, probably far less common today, is by exploiting official product standards. A company supplying the UK Ministry of Defence many years ago with a unique product enjoyed secure business over a number of years because it was protected by a British Standard written around it. The customer regularly ordered to that standard so that competitors were kept out. Margins were, in these circumstances, higher than average and repeat business was assured. Such a practice could, depending on the circumstances, be deemed illegal under today's competition laws, but it would certainly have been unethical if corrupt means (which was not the case) had been used to get the standard through in the first place. Furthermore, situations like this are as bad for the supplier as for the customer, breeding undue complacency and blunting the cutting edge that only competition can bring.

Price rings

It is a matter of debate whether price fixing is less common than it used to be. The highly-publicized cases that came to light in the 1990s generally concerned practices dating back to the 1970s and the 1980s. For example, 17 ready-mixed concrete companies were fined £8.37 million in 1995 for price-fixing arrangements from this period. An interesting aspect of this case was that some of the companies involved tried to pass the blame on to their employees on the grounds that they had acted contrary to company rules prohibiting such activities. This example raises serious ethical questions regarding employer–employee relationships, which are dealt with later in Chapter 6.

Formal price cartels are not only unethical and illegal, they are also unstable and can carry within them the seeds of their own destruction. For example, they can encourage new players to enter the market, attracted by the high prices to be obtained. Alternatively, there is always the danger that a participant in a price ring will break ranks. The motive for doing so might not be ethical at all, but if as a result the ring is broken and competition restored, then it can be said that the outcome is satisfactory.

For instance, it could happen that a group of local manufacturers and importers, all household names, have a market-sharing arrangement for an annual tender to a large state-controlled entity. They meet once a year to agree on what prices each will quote, the lowest figure being allocated to the participant whose turn it is to get the business on each product line required. One year it is the turn of one of the importers to quote the lowest price for a useful share of the business, but the Chief Executive decides it does not suit him to do so. His supplies of the product required are limited and he knows the customer to be one of the worst payers in the country. So he offers to forego his share in return for a payment, cash down, from the competitor who would get it instead, which is readily agreed. So his company's cash flow benefits modestly at once, while the successful competitor has to wait a very long time for his rather larger profit on the business.

Or, as a second example, the leaders in an industry might meet informally from time to time in a hotel room to discuss matters of mutual interest, such as life in general, new developments, prices and availability of raw materials – and list prices. They have a troublesome competitor with a much lower cost base than theirs, which has been partly achieved by the exclusion of trades unions and products meeting minimum quality standards. At one such meeting they discuss what they might do to combat this competitor. The discussion is inconclusive, but one of the participants is shocked a day or two later to receive a tape recording of the whole meeting with the implied threat that if they do not back off, the whistle will be blown to the competition authorities. Realizing that their meeting has been bugged by the troublesome competitor, the participants quietly drop the idea of concerted action against it.

It would be naïve to think that such activities have not taken place in the past, and maybe some still do, but participants in such arrangements need to be as wary of their own competitors as of the rigours of the law.

Price competition can also be limited without formal arrangements between competitors. In markets where there are few players – effectively where oligopoly exists – prices can be set in a purely tacit manner without a single meeting or telephone call. Price leadership can be exercised, perhaps through a price increase put through by the largest competitor, with the others following gratefully. This may not be illegal, but is it immoral? Some might think so, whilst others would regard that as an unfair value judgment.

In some businesses, such as petrol retailing in the UK, there was no chance of comfortable price leadership exercised by the oil companies. The cut prices offered by the supermarket petrol chains took such a large slice of the market that some of the oil majors were forced to announce an absolutely legitimate policy of local price checks, thus enabling them to compete and try to maintain (or regain) market share. Although price wars of this kind may seem beneficial to the consumer in the medium term, the danger of course is that they can result in too many players withdrawing from the market, thus allowing prices to rise again.

The need for legal restraints

Business supports competition law more than most legislation governing its activity, because it is needed to secure the level playing field on which companies can compete with one another. Above all, business needs the law to be clear; business people need to know where they stand. Unfortunately, the law is all too often unclear because this is an extraordinarily difficult and complex subject for legislation and one that is often inadequately understood by both politicians and bureaucrats.

Even Milton Friedman, one of the main protagonists of minimum government intervention in the operation of the market, has been quite clear that the

15

control of monopolistic or cartel activity is one where legislation is essential, especially in Europe. Writing in *Capitalism and Freedom*, he said that in the 'continental tradition ... enterprises are free to do what they want, including the fixing of prices, division of markets, and the adoption of other techniques to keep out potential competitors'. Considering he was writing a full fifteen years after the signing of the Treaty of Rome (including the key Articles 85 and 86 on competition), this statement was seen by many Europeans as a somewhat prejudiced comparison with the stringent legislation in the US. Indeed, one of the problems internationally has been the resentment by the United States, where the restrictions are much tougher than elsewhere, that there was an uneven playing field between them and other countries. Within the European Union, Articles 85 and 86 of the Treaty of Rome and subsequent Regulations are by degrees ensuring uniformity of national legislation but, as is so often the case, there is a feeling that considerable differences remain in the level of enforcement by member states.

Many people, notably from consumer organizations, campaigned during the early and middle 1990s for competition law in the UK to be toughened up. In response, the government announced in 1996 that it would take steps to strengthen the law and also to bring it more into line with the competition provisions of the European Union. After the general election in 1997, there were delays in enactment as various options were reviewed by the incoming government. Business, as is so often the case in such instances, was concerned that all this would in the end result in poor and unnecessarily complex legislation. Indeed, this process showed the new government how difficult it is to legislate in the area and then enforce the law effectively.

For although it is likely that both the public and Parliament feel there are more misdeeds than there really are, there may still be situations where there are restrictive practices inadequately covered by the law or where the perpetrators rely on not being found out. It is in these instances that the ethical standards of the company are put to the test and where, in the last analysis, the individuals involved are faced with hard personal decisions because, in following their consciences, they might be putting their careers at risk. There is more on this in Chapter 6.

RESTRICTIVE PRACTICES IN THE PROFESSIONS

Some of the old restrictive practices in the professions in the UK and elsewhere originated from the genuine need to ensure that professional work was only carried out by properly qualified people. An essential aspect of such qualifications was commitment to standards of conduct that became formally codified over time. But this perfectly legitimate and ethical objective of the professional associations resulted in outsiders being excluded from certain types of work, while fixed rates of remuneration were established for specific tasks, such as conveyancing by solicitors or commission on selling houses by estate agents. Some professions also protected themselves more subtly by surrounding their members with professional mystique that was supported by impenetrable jargon (a favourite activity of computer gurus working on mainframes and later those involved with selling PCs and software).

In recent years the professional associations have moved rapidly from their original role as protectors of their members towards becoming self-regulators, the main object of which is to ensure high standards of ethical behaviour in dealing with clients while at the same time trying to protect their members from overprescriptive government regulation. The main purpose of this section of the book, therefore, is to give some examples of the practical and ethical benefits that have arisen as a result of the introduction of competition in the professions.

Some people still doubt that it is effective enough. Will Hutton, in *The State We're In*, wrote: '... accountants and solicitors are practised in charging their clients excessive amounts'. To what extent this is true and to what extent it is a matter of opinion must be left to the reader. If the perceptions of both journalists and some sections of the public are that professional fees are protected by restrictions in competition, then there is much to be said for making their codes of practice and how they actually operate better known. Furthermore, professional firms need to make sure they avoid breaches of their own codes and are seen to do so. In the last resort, it may be up to individuals to follow their personal consciences in such matters.

Solicitors

Solicitors in England and Wales used to be bound by a system of scale fees (effectively a price cartel) for certain types of work, principally conveyancing. The system was enforced by the Law Society and ensured that price competition could not exist. Scale fees were abolished in the 1970s – well after the legislation on Resale Price Maintenance was enacted for consumer goods – and the rules on conveyancing practice and who could undertake it were substantially relaxed. Charges for conveyancing continued to be governed (as all other types of legal work) by the statutory regulations that provide guidelines on criteria (including time spent, importance to the client, the complexity of the work, the amount of money involved, and the like) for arriving at appropriate fees. In practice, the criteria can have varying effects: a small firm lacking relevant expertise might require a longer time to perform a task than would a large firm with greater resources, but the small firm might have much lower costing rates based on more modest overheads.

17

Professional rules now require a solicitor to quote for a job in advance, if so requested. With the client in a better position to 'shop around' on the basis of competitive quotations, competition on price is assured and quality of work is probably enhanced. However it is still against the rules for a practitioner to fail to disclose and explain the basis on which the charges are established or to claim they are based on Law Society guidelines which the firm does not properly define.

It is interesting that the Law Society went through agonizing internal discussions in the mid-1990s when trying to decide to what extent it was 'a trade union or a regulator', as a journalist at *The Times* put it. The need for more self-regulatory rules, codes and standards put a great deal of pressure on smaller firms, the margins of which had already been squeezed by increased competition from the larger firms that were better able to take the new rules on board. There is a clear ethical dilemma here, in that the higher standards needed to protect the consumer could restrict competition in the marketplace, with the particular effect of reducing the number of small local firms. This shows just how difficult it is to resolve many problems of this kind.

Accountants

Accountants, as a profession, have shared many experiences similar to those described for solicitors above. While at one time clients were rather in awe of their auditors and the technical mysteries surrounding their work, they now negotiate hard on fees, so that competition is more effective than it used to be.

The bodies representing the accountancy profession are now, like the Law Society, more concerned with self-regulation, designed to achieve high standards of ethics and professional competence. It is the norm for the larger firms to have their own internal manuals of ethics, in which the key requirements are integrity and the preservation of independence and objectivity. The codes of practice of the profession appear to be more concerned with competing for business in a fair manner and correct behaviour vis-à-vis clients than with any overt prohibition of market sharing or price agreements between firms, which are proscribed under the law.

However, self-regulation is not regarded as an adequate safeguard by some critics. For example, the left-wing Labour MP Austin Mitchell contemptuously dismissed self-regulation as 'chaps regulating chaps', a reference to an allegedly cosy and toothless old boy network. He claimed that self-regulation had not exposed early enough the fraud by Robert Maxwell or at BCCI or Barlow Clowes. Furthermore, he asserted that although accountancy bodies are required by law to monitor the quality of auditors' work, they confine themselves to checking 'mechanistic compliance with auditing standards'. He failed to recognize that 'quality' in auditing can be highly subjective, while conformity to standards can be checked in a more objective manner.

Professional accountants can be profoundly irritated by such attacks but, as is pointed out continually in this book, perceptions can become more important than objective facts when policy is being formulated by governments.

It is even more important for accountants to recognize the misgivings of their clients. Mergers of the largest firms can give rise to such concerns. In 1997 there were six very large international firms, most of which were themselves the result of earlier mergers. When two of them announced their intention to merge, followed by two others, it was then speculated that the remaining two might feel they had to follow suit, thus reducing their number to three only. Some of their clients showed concern that competition between the biggest and best-resourced international firms would be severely reduced, with a consequential restriction of choice for clients. The chairman of the One Hundred Group of leading UK finance directors was reported as saying: 'We don't see the advantage from the customers' point of view and we are also concerned about reduced competition.' While some such mergers are concluded successfully, they are sometimes more easily talked about than achieved, perhaps in recognition that, in part at least, those involved can be faced with the loss of some very large clients. It is known that many clients quite reasonably insist that their auditors do not work for any competitor in the same line of business.

Of course, clients can cause problems for their auditors as well. For example, creative accounting poses a real challenge for auditing firms. The Accounting Standards Committee was set up by the profession early in the 1970s to deal with perceived mischief at that time by setting standards and offering broad guidance. This was replaced in 1990 by the wholly independent Accounting Standards Board (see Appendix G), which further developed standards based on principles rather than detailed rules in order to deal with areas of difficulty. Even so, some finance directors found these rules burdensome. The auditor could find himself with a stark challenge: either use his expert knowledge of accounting standards to find a way round the rules and allow his client to do what it wanted, or risk losing the client. Reputable auditors argue that they handle this properly, but it is clearly an area of potential conflict of interest and temptation.

Estate agents

Estate agents dealing in the housing market in the UK are in a very different situation from the other professions covered in this section, because a large proportion – some say as many as seventy per cent – have no formal qualifications at all. Not having passed the necessary examinations, they cannot be members of the two main professional bodies, the Royal Institute of Chartered Surveyors and the Incorporated Society of Valuers and Auctioneers, and are therefore not subject to the codes of conduct of these bodies.

So, fixed fees having been abolished in the early 1970s and the Estate Agents Act 1979 having laid down that clients must be given a quotation in advance of the fees to be charged and the details of service to be provided, there is no doubt that competition is assured. However, the qualified members of the profession feel that such competition, especially from the unqualified, can put the consumer at risk. In contrast to most other trades, the consumer only relatively infrequently enters the market, so that reputation often depends on personal recommendation (or word of mouth warnings) and the principle of *caveat emptor* becomes paramount.

Agents' interests are not necessarily the same as those of their clients. The latter are concerned with achieving the highest possible selling price, within an acceptable time frame, while the former want the highest price commensurate with the lowest selling costs, which may mean the client does not get as good a deal as he might. Less ethical agents might tempt clients to instruct them by giving them exaggerated estimates of how much a house will fetch. Then there are cases of unscrupulous agents who act on behalf of buyers by cutting out higher bids, while also acting for sellers, and taking commissions from both.

Conflicts of interest may not only be confined to the smaller, unqualified 'cowboys' in the business. In some cases major corporate chains of estate agents are part of highly reputable public companies and yet there can still be conflicts of interest, in that they are not only in the business of buying and selling houses, but also selling mortgages and insurance policies. Difficult as this competition can be for independent agents, it is fair, provided sales commissions themselves are not being used as loss leaders to hook clients into paying artificially high prices for other services.

The perception of many people is that they are at a disadvantage, whatever the state of the market. When the housing market was paralysed from the late 1980s to the mid-1990s, the desperate hunt for business tempted some estate agents to adopt unscrupulous practices, to the detriment of the public. Then, when the market began to recover, competition among prospective buyers became so fierce that there was plenty of scope for exploitation.

In theory, the Office of Fair Trading (OFT) has powers under the 1979 Act to ban estate agents indulging in unethical activities; in practice, consumer bodies feel that the mechanisms for doing so have been shown to be cumbersome and ineffective. The establishment of the Ombudsman for Estate Agents, supported by the two main professional bodies and the National Association of Estate Agents, was aimed at raising ethical standards among members of those bodies, but while membership remained voluntary there was still plenty of room for the unscrupulous to operate. Hence consumer bodies and some of the independent estate agents continued to see no solution other than increased government regulation.

Banks

The standard interest rates charged by the banks up to the early 1970s meant that competition was limited to the helpfulness of the manager and the quality of advice given – not unimportant, but still not much use to borrowers with inadequate collateral who were not regarded as acceptable risks. Such borrowers were often forced into the secondary market where rates were much higher which, it can be argued, was a correct market-based outcome but in many cases it only further increased their indebtedness. The introduction of variable rates and the increase in the number of competitors as building societies and others moved into banking have given borrowers much more choice and the lenders more opportunity to choose clients by varying the rates offered.

However, the massive rationalization which has taken place in the banking system (partly for competitive reasons) has meant that many consumers are less happy than they used to be with the service they get from some banks, especially at a personal level. Small local branches have been closed with little concern for the convenience and accessibility of the alternatives offered and, at the same time, an impersonal business centre is perceived by many customers as less friendly than the old-fashioned bank manager. Competition comes into play when clients leave their traditional banks because they believe they can get better service or lower costs elsewhere, especially from providers of telephone banking (which offers considerable advantages to some), the former building societies or even the grocery chains now providing financial services.

In 1992 a code of practice, *Good Banking*, was published on behalf of banks, building societies and credit card issuers, to address their relations with personal customers, and it was revised in 1994 and 1997. It was described as 'a voluntary Code which allows competition and market forces to operate to encourage higher standards for the benefit of customers'. The governing principles of the Code were to set out standards of good banking practice, ensuring fair and reasonable dealings with customers (both depositors and borrowers), who needed to have a clear understanding of how their accounts were operated. The code made provision for the proper handling of customer complaints, with appeal, if necessary, to the independent Banking Ombudsman and other bodies dealing with leasing and consumer credit.

These principles are incorporated in the individual codes of the banks and building societies themselves, which also cover relationships with business clients, many of whom complained to the government in the early 1990s that they were not getting the full benefits of cuts in interest rates. On investigation, it was found that only seventy per cent of the borrowers had received the full reduction, which critics regarded as cause for concern, but one senior banker thought was 'pretty good', as customers had no more right to a more favourable rate than they had to paying the best possible price when buying any product. However, while competition does come into play in such instances, some people find it rather more difficult to move to another lender than, say, to a different car dealer!

In truth, few consumers know that regulations require the banks to maintain a minimum ratio between capital and risk assets and that they therefore have to take that obligation into account when making decisions on pricing (such as interest rates) or costs (including branch closures). This means that while most companies in other businesses can opt for lower profit to gain competitive advantage, banks may not if it inhibits the maintenance of their capital ratios at the levels laid down.

Ethics have become a competitive issue in themselves in the UK banking sector. The Co-operative Bank made its own ethical stance on investment and lending a major feature of its advertising in the mid-1990s, and NatWest was the first bank in the world to start issuing environmental reports (in 1993). This showed that both banks recognized not only that their operations and lending had a significant ethical and environmental impact, but that to do so was good for their overall reputation. (On this aspect of competition, see also Chapter 7.)

THE UTILITIES

While there have been plenty of political disagreements over the years about many aspects of the privatization of utilities in the UK, there is one area where there has been little argument, namely the desirability of introducing competition. Discussion has focused mainly on how to make it work. The key problem in this context has been the transition period between the transfer of state monopolies into the private sector before competition could be brought into play, not least because it was characterized by ethically-controversial features, notably what critics saw as the excessive remuneration of some directors and a highly politicized argument about the 'right' level of reward to shareholders.

The role of the regulators in this transition period is fraught with ethical dilemmas, in that excessive concern to ensure a fair deal for consumers often results in severe penalties for other stakeholders, especially employees and shareholders. The consequent power and influence of the regulators (which are not always matched by superhuman wisdom and ability) only emphasizes the importance of effective competition – but it is the practical difficulty of achieving this in the case of utilities that makes the role of the regulators necessary in the first place.

Water

In this context, water, as a natural monopoly, is the most difficult to deal with. Some limited local competition is possible, but more can only be achieved with the desirable but highly costly construction of local grid systems. The virtual impossibility of constructing a national grid means competition will remain imperfect and the regulator's role may be permanent.

Gas

The supply of gas has become subject to much controversy in the later 1990s after the creation of the separate distribution company Transco, owned by British Gas (BG), through which consumers would gradually be able to choose gas from various other sources in competition with the original monopoly supplier, BG itself. The battle with the powerful regulator over consumer price reductions has raised important questions relating to the balance of interest of the company (regarding investment), the shareholders (regarding share price and dividends) and employees (regarding jobs). Meanwhile consumers become more confused as new suppliers of gas appear on the scene, offering lower prices but in many cases little or no service. The relatively simple days of dealing with a single but expensive supplier are over.

Electricity

The UK electricity industry has also had its distribution system separated from the generators, though in this case there had been an element of foreign competition for some time in the shape of imports of electricity from France. With some distributors moving back into generation and into gas and other sources of energy, future competition is likely to be among a wide range of firms (including BG) that are delivering various energy services but that are no longer clearly distinguishable from each other by the products they sell.

Telecommunications

Competition in telecommunications was established in the UK in the early 1990s far more easily than the foregoing, with progressive price and service benefits to the consumer in a rapidly expanding and diversified market, the UK market leader, British Telecom (BT), aiming to become an increasingly important player on the world stage as overseas competitors move into its own home market.

There is no doubt at all that the consumer has benefited from lower prices and a wider choice of products than ever before but, as in the case of gas, has had to work harder in order to achieve those benefits because of the confusing and complicated competitive price structures on offer from different suppliers. There is no ethical problem here: the consumer has to make more effort than previously to reap the rewards available from increased competition.

The postal service

Consumers are already benefiting from some competition in postal services, ranging from couriers to electronic mail, which shows that privatization is not necessarily needed for competition to be introduced, though even if governments are willing to allow others to compete with them they are usually notoriously bad at it.

The fear that a universal postal service could be jeopardized by letting in other players prevented the UK's Conservative government from privatizing the Royal Mail in the same way that it had its much larger offspring, British Telecom. After the 1997 election, the new Labour government was torn between appreciation of the Royal Mail as a cash cow for the Treasury and concern about the effect on it in the future from foreign competition, the new technologies and the changing needs of its customers, particularly business. In the context of this book, the question of ownership of a national postal service is not crucial. What matters ethically is the provision of the service required by all sections of the community at acceptable costs. The achievement of this by the introduction of competition with built-in safeguards is far from easy, but the worst option was to do nothing and hope for the best.

Conclusion on utilities

Those running utilities have to recognize their central obligation to serve the public with integrity. In moral and in practical terms, because of the very nature of their businesses, these obligations are seen by consumers to be greater than those of retailers of food and clothing, or even financial services. Whatever the truth of the matter, there has been a public perception that in some cases inadequate service has been accompanied by excessively high rewards both to management and shareholders. Consequently it was not altogether surprising that there were no street demonstrations against the UK government's 1997 'windfall tax' on the utilities.

OTHER PUBLIC SERVICES

Is it ethically right to introduce business-style competition and market forces into public services, whether they remain fully or partially in the public sector? Charles Handy, in his book *The Hungry Spirit*, published in 1997, certainly did not think so. Acknowledging that the market is a 'wonderful discipline' for businesses 'with its built-in incentives and penalties, a spur to invention and improvement', he added that many die in the process. 'But schools, hospitals and welfare agencies cannot be allowed to die when they are inefficient, because there might not be any others nearby to replace them.' Not everyone would fully agree with this point. For example, in the highly controversial case of health services, the benefits of competition between the state and private sectors ought to result in greater efficiency and therefore better service to the consumer by both. But of course this leaves the moral problem of a two-tier service unresolved.

As Handy indicated, there are other areas of activity in the public sector where the introduction of market forces and competition are seen to be controversial. Education, which like public health should be essentially non-profit-making, can benefit from some aspects of competition, so that consumers can exercise some choice and thereby see improvements in the service provided.

There are other services, such as defence and the police, where there is (and should be) far less scope for competition, though even in the case of the latter, private security firms are in a sense competing with them at least in some of the areas of crime prevention rather than the enforcement of the law. Certainly there seems to be no moral problem in both the armed services and the police deriving real practical benefits from putting out many of their support services to competitive tender.

Neville Cooper, former Chairman of the Institute of Business Ethics, said in this context: 'Imperfect human nature needs a stimulus to do better and try harder. Comparative statistics are one way of introducing a sense of competition – between regions, departments or whatever.' One of the worries of those who distrust the exercise of competition in public services is that the pursuit of self-interest seems opposed to the very concept of public service. Even if they grudgingly accept the benign influence of the 'invisible hand' in the wider world of commerce, they feel that it somehow does not belong in the public service context.

TRADE PROTECTIONISM

No study of ethical aspects of competition can ignore this important and highly technical and complex subject. There are times when governments and many of those who vote for them are in favour of tariffs and other measures to protect domestic industries from foreign competition. This point of view often claims the moral high ground because jobs are preserved in the face of unfair competition from low wage countries with little or no social security provision, where children are exploited or where forced labour is used in production and human rights are generally denied. Add to that inadequate environmental protection, and the case can appear very strong indeed.

However, advocates of free and open trade take the view that protectionism, because it limits competition between individual countries or trading blocs, results in severe penalties to consumers, in inefficient allocation of resources and prevention of an effective international division of labour. Perhaps the strongest ethical argument of all is that in the case of third-world countries trade is greatly preferable to aid. Advocates of this view made sure it was a key issue in the marathon Uruguay Round of international trade negotiations that were finally concluded in 1994. Throughout the Round there were endless arguments about fair trade and about that most Anglo-Saxon of concepts, the level playing field. (It was notable that most people who used the expression were in fact advocating the need for protectionism of some kind against the allegedly unfair trading practices of others.)

The World Trade Organization (WTO), which succeeded the General Agreement on Tariffs and Trade (GATT) on completion of the Round, exists to foster free trade. Prior to the organization's first ministerial meeting in Singapore in 1996, its first Director General, Renato Ruggiero, spoke about the use of forced and child labour in the following terms:

> It is necessary to clarify whether this is a concern for human rights or for competitivity. I am certainly aware of the sensitivities on both sides of the issue. In my view, protectionism is no answer to concerns about labour standards. On the other hand, I believe it should be equally accepted that countries should not improve their competitive position through deliberately exploiting vulnerable sections of the labour force.

This is a key point. International competition should not be limited by moral considerations which are best dealt with by means other than protectionism.

Advocates of the European Union's Common Agricultural Policy (CAP) are mainly to be found among farmers (especially the smaller and more vulnerable among them) and among the politicians who rely on their votes. For the rest of the population there is a double cost, namely taxpayers' money used for intervention (including meeting fraudulent claims) and the higher cost of food due to the denial of the benefits of free competition from world markets. In the 1980s and early 1990s, that higher cost was roughly the same as the cost of the ill-fated poll tax to the average British family. People demonstrated in the streets against the latter, but the majority are blissfully unaware of the former. There are few better examples of a situation where views on the ethics of limiting competition are dependent on who one is and what one does, but in practical terms farmers have known for a long time that it is wise not to become too reliant on benefits that are likely to be transitory.

Public policy on trade issues of this kind is usually developed for reasons of expediency, yet there are important ethical considerations to be taken into account. Business people (including farmers) seldom consider these ethical aspects when demanding protection and seeking to limit competition, which is against the interest of the public at large. When protection is sought on moral grounds that are either spurious or better dealt with through other aspects of public policy, they are on even weaker ground.

A feature of the late 1990s in the EU, and in the UK in particular, is the constant theme that it is essential to achieve competitiveness with the rest of the world and especially with the countries of the Asian Rim. Interestingly, there is much less demand for old-fashioned protection (which would be contrary to the GATT agreement) and much more concentration on the need for internal action to make competitiveness possible. This means, for example, that the EU tries to negotiate trade deals with reciprocity on social protection attached. This in turn begs the question of whether or not the benefits of the so-called 'social market economies' in Europe, however desirable in themselves, may be a threat to competitiveness, and whether, as they are essential to funding social services in the first place, they should be maintained.

INTELLECTUAL PROPERTY

Patent and trade-mark rights are an essential means of conferring ownership on those responsible for their own creations, whether these are technical inventions, brand names, books, software or music. This is an exclusive property right; competitors may face very real problems if the quality of the patented product is outstanding. To cover extreme cases, there are provisions in competition law to prevent the abuse of a dominant position in any one area. In the EU, for example, intellectual property rights may not be used to divide up the territory of the single market. Owners of intellectual property rights, whatever they are, reject absolutely allegations that they are exempted from competition law and thus benefit from feather-bedding. However, there are cases where patents and trade marks can be misused as an unethical means of limiting competition, for example when they are either trivial in nature or of dubious legality.

Patent Protection

The arguments in favour of patent protection are very powerful indeed, especially for products requiring heavy R&D budgets and long lead times, including product testing, before they can be launched on to the market. Patent laws are absolutely essential if those responsible for the invention are to realize a reasonable return in their investment and, indeed, if others are to have the confidence to follow them in developing further products.

Sometimes a patented product can be so good that it seems there is a *de facto* limitation to competition until the patent expires, which hurts competitors but is still perfectly ethical. One example was the steel radial tyre, for which Michelin had patent protection until the 1970s. The most significant advantage over their rivals' textile radial tyres (patented by Pirelli and also made under licence by others) was that the steel version gave much higher mileage. In most cases Michelin were able to charge higher prices for their superior product (while many dealers were able to sell on to users with lower discounts), but as a result were still able to achieve substantial increases in market share in most, if not all, of the countries where they operated.

The strength of Michelin's position at that time is illustrated by the experience of the exasperated manager of an overseas selling company of a rival manufacturer, who received a batch of tyres which he rejected on quality grounds. After he had returned them to the factory, he was asked what could be done to put matters right. He jeopardized his career by saying the next batch should be both round and preferably carry the Michelin name. It was inevitable that all tyre manufacturers switched to steel as soon as Michelin's patents ran out.

In no industry are there more important principles of patent protection than in pharmaceuticals, nor greater ethical counter-arguments, which are put forward in favour of the poorer sections of society in the world having access to cheaper generic drugs. Such arguments could amount to a form of moral blackmail, but in more practical terms it would be folly to starve the geese that lay the golden eggs.

Trade mark protection

Owners of heavily promoted brands with trade mark protection are no less adamant that this limitation of competition is absolutely vital to them. Understandably, the producers of Champagne or Coca-Cola go to enormous lengths and cost to protect their names and their brands. It may be ethical to restrict competition in this way, but the various means of doing so can range from the generally acceptable to the downright unethical.

Development by supermarkets of their own brands, which are usually sold at lower prices than the equivalents from the manufacturers, is highly unwelcome to the latter because it reduces their market share, but is completely legitimate. The consumer has to decide, case by case, whether the cheaper own-branded product is really value for money or not, and in many cases the consumer may still prefer the original.

Sometimes the own-branded product is identical to the original except for the packaging. For instance, a UK factory making a product with a nationally known brand name churned out thirty other retailers' own-name brands on the same production line. They were identical apart from the bags in which they were supplied. The retailers' brands were almost invariably sold cheaper than the original brand in the shops. Although consumers could not know the product specification inside the packing was identical, it was left to them to choose whether to buy the nationally advertised brand with its prestige name rather than the retailer's own brand.

The case quoted above was not for a luxury product. There are, however, cases where the higher prices charged for such products are often challenged by consumers as unjust. This can lead some of them to feel that they are justified in becoming party to buying illegal or morally questionable alternatives (see the section on counterfeiting in Chapter 5).

'EXCESSIVE' COMPETITION

One of the paradoxes of celebrating competition is that sometimes there can be too much of it, so that it defeats its own object by going too far. This is when special novel factors arise which disturb the normal function of competition and threaten to reduce the number of participants in the market, or have an adverse effect on the interests of the consumer. Many, but not all, of the examples of this phenomenon that are given below are to be found in the transport industry.

The UK bus industry

Following deregulation, there were too many buses in urban areas from rival companies chasing too few customers on the same routes. (This was in contrast to the vicious circle in rural areas, where there were too few buses chasing ever fewer passengers who were forced to use their cars because of the poor service.) This is more a practical than a moral issue, though it is obviously unethical for the streets to be unnecessarily congested, pollution increased and resources wasted. It was also undoubtedly unethical for some of the stronger players to try to put their weaker competitors out of business through predatory pricing.

On the other hand, it was almost too easy for new entrants to get into the market with second-hand vehicles. Competition on the main routes was so fierce that old vehicles were not replaced in due time, which created additional safety and pollution hazards. A return to regulation appeared ethically necessary, but ironically this favoured the larger operators who were already moving towards market dominance and attracting the attention of the Monopolies Commission.

Air transportation

In the United States, deregulation of air transportation resulted in the short term in a vicious price war that favoured consumers. Ultimately, however, there was an inevitable reduction in the number of competitors and increasing worries about the safety of some of the older aircraft operated by the smaller companies. In Europe the liberalization of air transportation was the subject of intensive lobbying in the 1980s by certain carriers, such as the privatized British Airways and the liberal KLM, but not viewed so kindly by the then heavily-subsidized, state-owned airlines such as Air France. There is no doubt that the relaxation of the monopoly of national carriers operating flights between each other's home territory is greatly in the interest of consumers, but legal and ethical questions can arise if competition becomes too cutthroat, and safety is then put at risk.

A new form of competition in the later 1990s was the appearance of small, independent, low-overhead airlines offering cheap, no-frills services without reducing safety. So successful were they in creating what was in effect a new market segment that some of the larger, well-established airlines felt they could no longer ignore it. This raises some interesting ethical questions relating to large companies becoming involved in niche markets created by small, innovative ones, which resent the intrusion. The 'ethical' question raised by the smaller companies is obviously whether the larger companies are competing fairly, avoiding predatory pricing and cross-subsidization from other activities.

The decision by British Airways (BA) in 1997 to set up an independent subsidiary called Go to operate a cheap, no-frills service from the following spring evoked furious reaction from the smaller airlines already in the business. One of them, easyJet, took out a full-page advertisement in the press demanding intervention from the Brussels competition authorities on the grounds that BA had admitted that the new company would be losing money until the third year. It accused BA of 'acting as a dominant airline willing to lose unlimited sums of money competing with substantially smaller airlines that could be driven out of business in the process. It seems to us like a textbook case of abuse of dominant position under Article 86 of the EC Treaty.' It went on to list the smaller airlines that BA had either taken over or allegedly tried to put out of business. BA for its part made it clear that the new airline really would stand alone financially and that it would compete not on price but by offering a better service than its smaller rivals.

On the face of it, there is no ethical problem in a large company entering a market in this way, provided it competes fairly. Smaller airlines will no doubt continue to regard this as predatory behaviour because they feel vulnerable in such circumstances.

Shipping

Shipping provides an interesting example of a formal arrangement to regulate competition. The shipping lines that are members of 'liner conferences' agree on the frequency of sailings, the freight capacity to be available, and standard tariffs. Unfettered competition might lead to lower prices for individual shipments, but could also lead to disruption and uncertainty in the provision of the service.

For example, lines shipping new crops from the tropics might race to offer the first sailing at the start of a new season. That is fine for the first boat away and for the owners of its cargo and also for other ships which can achieve full loads at the height of the season. However, vessels might later on have to wait to find cargo, which is expensive, and customers with cargo at subsequent ports of call might be disappointed. Alternatively, perishable goods that arrived too late to catch the last cluster of sailings might find no available vessel for weeks and end up rotting on the quayside.

Such considerations have persuaded the European Union to permit liner conferences on strict terms. Even the United States has decided that the benefits of liner conferences outweigh the competitive disadvantages and permits their operation, albeit under strict regulation by the Federal Maritime Commission.

Ferries

The short sea route across the English Channel provides perhaps the most interesting case of 'excessive' competition, posing a number of ethical problems.

Before the Channel Tunnel opened to traffic in 1996, this was one of the most expensive ferry crossings in the world in terms of price per mile. The price competition that followed the opening and the fifty per cent increase in capacity was greatly to the advantage of consumers in the short term. However both Eurotunnel (which by 1995 was technically bankrupt and supported only by a suspension of interest payments) and the ferries began to feel the pinch in a big way, in spite of very strong growth in the total market. Moreover, the ferry companies had hanging over them the likelihood of additional regulations because of the need to improve passenger safety, which could result in their being forced to make very substantial capital investment in bulkheads. The lengthened loading and unloading times involved could also affect their competitiveness.

In 1996 two of the three ferry companies, P&O and Stena, were still prevented from rationalizing their services because of undertakings not to do so dating from 1979. As there was no question of the tunnel being allowed to close, the ferry companies welcomed the government decision in July 1996 to allow them to discuss how they might work together. The decision was also welcomed by Eurotunnel. Three months later, P&O and Stena announced their intention to merge on this route only. Consumer organizations were immediately indignant, saying that prices would rise, ignoring the fact that the previous situation of cut-price fares was only a honeymoon and could not continue indefinitely.

The concern here was the usual one: on the Dover–Calais route, the two companies would become the largest operator above the water. The European Commission's competition authorities and the UK government held up clearance because of fears that there would be inadequate ring-fencing of the Dover–Calais route from other routes served by the two companies separately, and also possibly cross-subsidization. In fact, the competition authorities' decisions were almost irrelevant, because it was clear that, if the merger had not been allowed to go ahead, there was always the danger that one of the partners would walk away and the other would then take up a large proportion of its market share.

A market served in several ways is one market: a dominant position in part of it is normally only considered anti-competitive if that dominance is abused. After all, the tunnel has one hundred per cent of its part of the market; it would take a crazy bureaucrat indeed to insist on another tunnel being built to ensure more competition. In fact, competition continues to be very fierce on the cross-Channel route and the worries of consumer groups would appear to have been exaggerated.

The book trade

In the book trade the extent of competition has proved to be controversial, and ostensible ways of increasing it could have the reverse effect. There has always been intense competition among publishers, among authors and among booksellers. However, until relatively recently the Net Book Agreement (NBA) permitted a restriction on price competition among booksellers. Publishers were legally permitted to set minimum prices on their books as a means of encouraging booksellers to stock a wide range of titles, including slow movers that involve both higher cost and risk to them than is the case with best-sellers. Such availability was also seen to be in the interest of the public.

The NBA came under attack particularly from one leading bookseller, Dillons, the most rapidly growing chain of bookshops in Britain in the late 1990s, which wanted to discount prices by using the higher margins it enjoyed from its buying power as a major customer of the publishers. This opened up a fascinating debate on the public interest between price competition and wide product availability, particularly of a cultural product involving a constant flow of new titles. In 1995 the NBA was abandoned (although in theory it still existed for a while longer) under pressure from the major players competing for market share. Ironically, by then Dillons had so overreached itself that it nearly collapsed and was taken over by Thorn-EMI.

The free-market view of this was that the consumer would benefit from discounting and that the market would expand. Supporters of the NBA argued that without it large retailers would be able to increase market share by discounting best-sellers, and that other retailers such as large supermarkets would also cream off the market for popular paperbacks; this would be to the detriment of booksellers stocking wide ranges and reduce the availability of many titles to the public. Not only would this increase the domination of the market by the major players, it would also drive smaller, more varied businesses and more new quality titles out of the market. It was expected that this would mirror the experience of small retailers in other trades, thus raising some familiar ethical questions in the minds of those worried by too much dominance of the bigger retailers. In practice, it was easy for both sides of the argument to produce evidence to support their views.

Pharmacies

The pharmacy trade was a case not unlike that of the book trade. Up to 1996 resale price maintenance (RPM) had been retained on over-the-counter drugs, the last of such arrangements in the UK since RPM was abolished on most products in 1970.

Grocery supermarkets, led by Asda, began to sell standard medicaments at cut prices, sometimes under their own brand names, a move which was seen as an additional service to the public. Small pharmacies, however, reacted strongly, arguing that the local service they provided by selling drugs under prescription could be reduced if they were deprived of too much of their bread-and-butter business in the products sold by the supermarkets. The decision by the OFT to refer the price maintenance arrangement to the Restrictive Trade Practices Court was hailed by Asda's Chief Executive as a 'victory for ordinary working people and their families', but it remains to be seen how many small pharmacies will be forced to close if the OFT's move is upheld.

Of course, competition usually results in some businesses going to the wall, but there is always a stronger moral backlash if they are small, provide a valuable service to a local community and are deemed to be the victims of the big battalions.

Conclusion on 'excessive' competition

The above examples of 'excessive' competition illustrate three common ethical themes, as follows.

- Strong price competition from the larger players in a market can appear beneficial to the consumer, but can result in a reduction in the number of local suppliers from whom the consumer can buy.

- There need to have safeguards against cross-subsidization from other businesses by the larger players and from predatory pricing, both of which can operate at the expense of smaller competitors.

- 'Excessive' competition and price wars can lead to reduced quality of products and services or, more seriously, reduced observance of safety standards.

Chapter 3

Honest? Decent? Truthful?

No study of the ethics of competition can ignore the key role of advertising. There are few ethical aspects of business about which such extreme views are held. The less competition there is, as was the case in Communist societies, the less need there is for advertising; conversely, the more competition there is, the more important it becomes.

The question is whether the familiar case in favour of advertising is ethical or not. There are four main justifications for it:

- advertising plays an important role in providing information to consumers on products that are available, where they can be obtained and what they will cost;

- the product being sold must be distinguished from its rivals, thus helping consumers to exercise choice;

- advertising is vital in establishing brands that consumers can recognize and then rely upon;

- volume can be built up by creating demand, especially for new products, which in turn can lead to lower prices.

Sir Gordon Borrie, when Director General of The Office of Fair Trading, said in 1991: 'Greater competition will bring better choice and better value for consumers. No one has yet produced a better instrument than lively competition to produce satisfied consumers.' This quotation was taken up by Patricia Mann, a director of J Walter Thompson and Editor of *Consumer Affairs*:

> There is no better evidence of the lively competition which produces satisfied consumers than advertising. It is the most visible sign of the constant competition between suppliers to win and keep consumers' custom for their goods and ser-

vices. As the dynamo of fair competition, advertising has substantial benefits for consumers: more choice, better value, more new and improved products and wider distribution for them so that they are readily accessible.

All these reasons appear to be ethically acceptable or, at worst, ethically neutral. Conversely, critics of advertising see the unethical side as follows:

- the information given in advertisements is not as objective as it should be, because it is provided by the advertiser and suitably hyped up by the copy-writers (an argument, carried to its logical conclusion, suggesting that all advertisements should be produced by independent consumer bodies);

- the way in which products are distinguished one from another is sometimes spurious, or even dishonest;

- the cost of establishing and then keeping brands in the minds of the public is far too high, adds unnecessarily to the price of the product and is wasteful;

- advertising creates demand, or even makes consumers think they have needs they had never dreamed of previously.

At present, the UK advertising industry's self-regulation is only aimed at the first three objections in the list above. However, the last is considered by many people to be especially valid in affluent societies where environmental damage is still increasing and when the gap between rich and poor in the world is still widening. This is an important moral question with important political implications.

The main point of this chapter is in line with the central theme of this book – namely that, as with other aspects of competition, advertising is justified providing it sticks to fundamental rules. There is nothing new in this. It may come as a surprise to some readers that the first international code of advertising practice was published in 1937 by the International Chamber of Commerce (ICC) with strong input from the UK. The idea of advertising having to be 'legal, honest, decent and truthful' has been around a long time. The Code has been updated four times since, while supplements on advertising to children and environmental product claims have been added. This is perhaps one of the most successful and extensively used self-regulatory codes the world has ever seen and it has been adapted for inclusion and development in the national codes of many countries.

In the UK these principles are upheld by the Advertising Standards Authority (ASA) for all advertising except on television, which is handled by the Independent Television Commission (ITC), and on commercial radio, which is covered by the Radio Authority.

The problem, as always, is that there are many 'grey areas' between what is banned by law, such as misleading advertising and certain specific products (tobacco, for instance, in an increasing number of countries) and what, often highly subjectively, exceeds the standards of honesty, decency and truthfulness set out in codes. So desperate are some companies to achieve sales, and some advertising agents to support them, that they very often get too close to the agreed limits. How far they are prepared to go depends on how advertisers and their agents see the possible damage to their own reputation, but the consciences of the individuals involved must also be brought to bear.

HONEST?

'Good products can be sold by honest advertising' is a truism attributed to David Ogilvy of Ogilvy & Mather. He is alleged also to have said that 'if you tell lies about a product, you will be found out'. This is not ethics but prudence; lack of honesty reflects on the advertiser, the agency, the business of advertising and above all on the product itself.

Under the heading of honesty, the ASA Code says: 'Advertisers should not exploit the credulity, lack of knowledge or inexperience of consumers.' Complaints about misleading advertisements are dealt with by the ASA under this article in the Code, which is backed up by a 1988 legal regulation administered by the Office of Fair Trading.

There are plenty of examples in most people's minds of advertisements which have sailed very close to the wind on such points, especially in relation to financial services, where there is a great deal of small print that members of the public fail to read and understand at their peril. This is why the regulators insist that the client has time after the purchasing decision to reread the small print and reconsider if necessary.

False or misleading product claims

False or misleading product claims can occur in media advertising or at the point of sale. The standard practice is an exaggerated claim, the ethics of which are highly subjective and of course dependent on the degree of exaggeration. Concealment of relevant information can of course be much more serious, even if it is not strictly illegal (as would be the case, for instance, where statutory safety warnings are withheld). In their enthusiasm to sell, marketing people need to rely on the explicit or implicit values of the company they work for, the codes of their profession and, ultimately, their own consciences.

The exploitation of illusion

The exploitation of illusion can also be highly subjective in ethical terms. For instance, packaging is often exaggerated to make the product look bigger or more significant than it is. In some cases, the justification is the need to protect it, but excessive use of packaging is also condemned on environmental grounds, so that penalties under EU directives reduce its cost-effectiveness.

Switch selling

Switch selling is another unethical practice, which takes many forms. The ASA Code prohibits advertisers from 'knocking' their own advertised product and trying to persuade the customer to buy a more expensive alternative. The Code also requires advertisers to make it known that stocks are limited. 'Hurry! hurry! hurry! while stocks last!' can get round this requirement and lead to another form of switch selling, which was prevalent in the 1970s and on which the Code is not specific enough, as given in the following example.

Well known products, for instance branded kitchen sinks, were offered in small 'box' ads in the press. When consumers sent their money, they were told that that particular product was sold out, but that an equivalent, 'which is just as good', could be supplied instead. In practice, the advertiser had only bought a few of the branded sinks and intended from the outset to sell the alternative on which he enjoyed a higher margin. In many such cases the customer was not disappointed, so the scam worked, even though there was always the remedy of demanding a refund or making a complaint to the ASA or the OFT.

Comparative advertising

Companies, in their efforts to compete, are often tempted to denigrate their competitors, or use 'knocking copy'. The Code is quite clear on this: 'Advertisers should not unfairly attack or discredit other businesses or their products.' The key word is 'unfairly' because comparative advertising is not only allowed in the UK but almost appears to be encouraged, subject of course to rules. The ASA in its Code again: 'Comparisons can be explicit or implied and can relate to advertisers' own products or to those of their competitors; they are permitted in the interests of vigorous competition and public information.' Because such comparisons should be 'clear and fair', this can still be dangerous ground, which was one of the reasons comparative advertising was earlier banned in several European countries including Belgium, Germany, Italy and Luxembourg. In this interesting ethical 'grey area', the European Union has now moved towards the UK's more relaxed position.

In September 1997 a Directive was published by the European Commission, allowing comparative advertising throughout the EU under the following conditions, namely that:

■ it is not misleading, and it compares only those goods or services meeting the same needs or intended for the same purposes;

- it does not create confusion in the market between the advertiser and a competitor or between advertisers' trade marks, trade names, other distinguishing marks, goods or services and those of a competitor;

- it does not discredit, denigrate or take unfair advantage of the trade marks, trade names etc of a competitor;

- while member states are not obliged to permit comparative advertising for goods and services on which they maintain or introduce total advertising bans, comparative advertising cannot otherwise be banned.

The Advertising Association quoted these conditions in its *Executive Briefs* of November 1997 and welcomed them as a 'genuinely liberalising measure designed to reduce barriers to advertising in the single market' and 'a rare example of genuine European Commission-led deregulation'. However, some companies take a more restrictive line on comparative advertising in accordance with their own values. For example, IBM specifically excludes such tactics in either its selling or its advertising; its philosophy is that the product must stand on its own merits.

DECENT?

The ASA Code is here concerned with advertisements that are likely to cause serious or widespread offence, taking into account the 'context, medium, audience, product and prevailing standards of decency'. This is a moving standard, offering plenty of problems to the regulators and facing busy executives with ethical decisions regarding the light in which they want their company to be seen.

The most obvious example is the gratuitous and often irrelevant exploitation of sexual images generally and especially those of women, that, as shown in Appendix A, so offends Muslims in particular. Standards may have improved in recent years, but this is not always because of the public codes of practice in operation. Responsible companies themselves have used appropriate restraint in accordance with the *mores* of the time and with due consideration for their reputation.

One simple example from the 1950s that shows this. The agency working for Dunlop in Sweden devised an advertisement showing an unclothed girl, facing the camera and holding a car tyre neatly in front of her so as to protect her decency. The caption read, simply: 'You should see our advertisements for bicycle tyres.' It was seen as relatively harmless and amusing but completely irrelevant and unworthy of the company, and so it was not used.

Some advertisers have nowadays come to realize that the use of sexual images that have nothing whatever to do with their products can be counter-productive, in that the consumer remembers the images, but has no idea what product is being promoted. There are exceptions to all such rules, one of the most notable examples being the Pirelli calendars, which are something of an art form and have achieved cult status.

As alluded to above, indecency in advertising tries to fulfil the ultimate objective – to draw attention to the product. However, in the mid-1990s voices were raised in protest from within the industry. Adrian Holmes, Chairman of the agency Lowe Howard-Spink, was reported by Graham Searjeant in *The Times* to have denounced 'the new unpleasantness, the new yobbishness – the new desire to shock the audience into taking notice by whatever means'. The audience of advertising people gave him a spontaneous round of applause.

An example from that time of 'going too far' relates to the shock tactics and bad taste of Benetton advertisements featuring death in various forms. It fell foul of the ASA code, while retailers in Germany claimed their offensiveness even lost them sales. According to a *Sunday Times* article, the company's defence was that the 'pictures should not be seen as advertisements, but as statements, images of social issues to raise public awareness and debate. Nothing could be further from Benetton's mind than selling jumpers.'

Andrew Brown, Director General of the Advertising Association, writing in support of Adrian Holmes, said: 'standards... represent best practice and contain a recognition of the responsibilities that are concomitant with the right of freedom of commercial speech. It is juvenile to reinterpret a belief in standards as an attack on creativity...'

The ASA Code says that 'Advertisers should not use shocking claims or images merely to attract attention,' but they 'may use an appeal to fear to encourage prudent behaviour or to discourage dangerous or ill-advised actions'. This enables insurance companies legitimately to play on people's fears about fire or burglary or acts of God, but their problem is to stand out from the crowd of very similar product claims and raise fears that the ASA says should not be 'disproportionate to the risk'.

Because attitudes to indecency in advertising are bound to vary enormously from generation to generation and are thus extremely subjective in the short term, opinions on what products should be advertised are obviously very diverse. Because of this, the ASA Code says: 'The fact that a particular product is offensive to some people is not sufficient grounds for objecting to an advertisement for it.' This principle is absolutely fundamental for those who believe in freedom in their debate with the prohibitionists who want to ban advertising of all products of which they themselves disapprove.

Advertising alcohol

One of the most widely discussed products falling into this category is alcohol.

The majority of adults accept both the product and the way it is advertised as ethical, provided it is consumed in sensible quantities and not before driving or working potentially dangerous machines. Indeed there is medical evidence that some drink – in moderation of course – is good for us as well as enjoyable.

No doubt the discussion will continue on whether ethics demand health warnings on advertising, or draconian restrictions such as the *Loi Evin* in France, where alcoholism is a big problem. There are also ethical and practical questions about levels of tax on alcohol that are prohibitive in Sweden, for example, and much higher in the UK than in many other members of the EU Single Market. There is a real paradox here. Those who wish to curb or ban alcohol welcome higher taxes, but these provide even more encouragement to the traffic of white vans across the Channel bringing cheaper alcohol into the UK from a country that has tougher advertising controls.

However much controversy there may be about the advertising of alcohol, society as a whole agrees that it is wrong for it to be directed at children, although in practice the arbitrary age watershed of eighteen for buying alcohol may be too high for some young people and too low for others. The problem is that while it is illegal to sell alcohol to children, it is almost impossible to prevent them drinking it.

The major British drinks producers demonstrated their recognition of the need to promote sensible drinking habits, responsible marketing, good retail practice and the avoidance of promotion or sale to under-18s, when they set up the Portman Group in 1989. This body's *Code of Practice*, published in 1996, was especially timely because of the controversy surrounding alcoholic soft drinks which are popularly known as 'alcopops'. Many of these have a similar alcohol content by volume to beer (between four and five per cent) and because of this they appeal especially to young adults and are indeed promoted to them.

The problem that arose was that they could also appeal to under-18s, who are attracted by their rather juvenile brand names (some of which have already been withdrawn) and also that confusion was likely to arise if such words as 'lemonade' or 'cola' appeared on the bottles. There were also complaints about the use on the labels of cartoon characters familiar to children. The industry's view was that these products were no more abused by under-18s than other alcoholic drinks and that the code as issued covered these points adequately, especially as steps were taken to reduce the confusion with soft drinks. (The market leader, 'Hooper's Hooch', had already replaced the word 'lemonade' with 'lemon' quite early on in the controversy and later relaunched the product with a lower sugar content and repackaged with a more adult image.)

However, some individuals and groups remained critical. Sales people were even accused of deliberately introducing alcopops in places where drugs were available to young people because of fears of competition from so-called 'recreational' products such as Ecstasy or worse. Many young people prefer soft drinks to alcohol as being less harmful.

Some people in the brewing industry took the view that the anti-alcohol lobby would never be satisfied. Their attitude was that alcopops were a perfectly legitimate alternative to beer or lager. Indeed there is not much difference between modern alcopops and old-fashioned shandies made from beer and lemonade or ginger beer, which have never attracted much criticism.

A report that a judge had condemned the makers of alcopops, after a 14-year-old boy had got drunk on alcoholic lemonade of some kind and cider and burned down a school, made the Home Secretary order an investigation into the sale, marketing and content of alcopops and resulted in other politicians demanding that 'something must be done'. Needless to say, this raised the usual arguments as to whether self-regulation was effective enough and threats of government intervention if it was not. Faced with all this controversy, some pub chains and supermarkets were forced to consider taking alcopops off their shelves and some did so on ethical grounds. One multinational, Grand Metropolitan (now Diageo), went so far as to state in its 1996 Annual Review that it did not make or market alcopops.

This shows just how difficult it is to establish whether the production and marketing of alcopops is an ethical way of competing or not. Those who have demonized the product have no doubt that it is scandalous, but others point out that young people can and do get hold of other wines, beers and spirits and that it is unfair to blame alcopops in particular for alcohol abuse by this age group.

This then raises the much wider question of alcohol advertising in general. The attitude of the UK Advertising Association in its *Executive Briefs* of November 1997 'encourages strict industry compliance with all existing laws and self-regulatory codes of practice in relation to advertising and promotion'. It goes on to say that 'there is no commercial advantage whatsoever to be gained from inappropriate or irresponsible advertising, or from promotions directed at children below the legal drinking age'. In short, the ethical imperative for advertisers is to support all efforts that prevent alcohol abuse or damage to health in all age groups.

Advertising tobacco

There are many parallels between the advertising of alcohol and that of tobacco, although the anti-smoking lobby has much wider support. Some people and politicians regard media advertising of tobacco as unacceptable and would like to see it banned in the EU. This view is not universally held, however, and the German Government, for example, is opposed to such a ban, *inter alia* on the grounds that it violates freedom of speech and improperly uses the harmonization provisions of the EU to cover a health issue.

41

As with alcohol, governments have great problems on this subject because revenues from taxes are so high that in many countries they comfortably exceed the additional burdens on health services ascribed to smoking. A study by the Centre for Health Economics at the University of York was reported in 1997 to have estimated costs to the National Health Service of a shocking £1.4 billion to £1.7 billion a year. This compares with an estimated duty raised on tobacco that year in excess of £10 billion, quite apart from all that the industry paid in corporation and income taxes and the overseas earnings from exports. It is hard for many people to accept statistics such as these, there being a perception that if all factors are taken into account, there may be a net cost to the nation from smoking. The debate will provide lawyers on both sides with plenty of work for many years to come.

Of course, the advertising industry has always opposed a ban on tobacco advertising and suffered instead its limitation and the use of health warnings. In this context it was said that when one country (*not* the UK) introduced such warnings for the first time, there was a run on the stocks of the remaining packets that did not show the dreaded advice in the belief that they were safer! Now that health warnings are not considered by authorities in many countries to be enough, it is perhaps appropriate to reiterate the argument of the advertising industry. In the words of the Advertising Association, the industry is 'professionally concerned only with advertising and its effects, rather than with approval or disapproval of particular products or services. Others in society must decide a product's legality but we must operate from the general principle that "*if it's legal to sell, it should be legal to advertise responsibly.*"'

In other words, the advertising industry takes the view that it, as well as the manufacturers of alcohol and tobacco, has the right of freedom of commercial speech, enshrined in article 10 of the European Convention on Human Rights, but it also recognizes that such a right carries responsibilities. The industry's corporate view is in line with the thesis of this book, namely that in areas where a business activity is legal there are also aspects where constraint has to be exercised on ethical grounds.

Creating unrecognized demand

Creating demand for products people did not know they needed is an aspect of advertising that has been touched on already and that some people consider indecent. Unsurprisingly, this is not addressed by codes. Creating demand for products and turning them into 'necessities' is a result of the skilful exercise of peer pressure. In an essay entitled 'The Dependence Effect', J K Galbraith wrote: 'As a society becomes increasingly affluent, wants are increasingly created by the process by which they are satisfied.' One of his concerns was that such artificial creation of consumption is often at the expense of necessary public services.

Nepal is one of the four or five poorest countries in the world. Even there, extensive advertising has made some non-essential products fashionable. An extreme example, which is often quoted critically by advocates of appropriate development in poor countries, is the advertising of Coca-Cola. Possibly reflecting Galbraith's views, the company linked some of its advertising to public service, by providing much-needed road signs carrying its logo.

In developed countries, there are now far more fundamental moral questions to be faced regarding the seemingly inexorable march of consumption fuelled by advertising. There are two mutually sustaining moral concerns here: the first is the warning, expressed in religious teaching, about excessive devotion to the acquisition and worship of worldly goods, and the second is the environmentalist argument about the damage that all this consumption is doing to the planet. These concerns are expressed mainly so far by religious ascetics and middle-class 'haves' who can afford to be 'green', but it is nevertheless an issue which society will have to face much more robustly in the twenty-first century.

'Sustainability' is already an overemployed word, considered further in Chapter 7. It has been used to support widely differing attitudes to our environmental problems but, once they are tackled, new and quite different market opportunities will emerge. For example, F A von Hayek wrote a stinging attack on Galbraith's essay quoted above, in which he suggested that the only basic needs of human beings are 'food, shelter and sex', and he then went on to say that it was very necessary to promote important non-basic needs such as music, painting and literature – which are, incidentally, much more environmentally sustainable than the hardware most of us seek to acquire. Whatever 'essential needs' are perceived to be, there will be competition to satisfy those needs and advertising will be called in to support it.

TRUTHFUL?

The ASA Code is brief and to the point: 'No advertisement should mislead by inaccuracy, ambiguity, exaggeration, omission or otherwise.' Again, these are highly subjective criteria.

Some false claims are closer to 'poetic licence' and need not be unethical at all: the invitation from Esso to 'put a tiger in your tank' is clearly false, but so obviously so that it does not mislead, provided the degree of sophistication of the target market is carefully taken into account! In contrast, false product claims that cannot be genuinely substantiated are usually a question of fact and are fairly easily dealt with. Even so, there are obvious words like 'best', which are often a matter of personal opinion (and thereby handled elegantly by Carlsberg when it claimed it was *probably* the best lager in the world').

One of the greatest problems here is the half truth, the statement that, in Alan Clark's immortal words, is 'economical with the *actualité*', such as the insurance policy which says it will pay hospital and surgical bills without stating that they will not be paid in full.

Advertisers of financial services do indeed have to be careful not to mislead in their zeal to beat competitors, as the following example shows. A leading UK insurance company offered an investment plan which would achieve 'market growth plus 40 per cent'. Half of a 300-strong consumer panel believed this meant that if the market rose ten per cent the plan would offer ten per cent plus forty per cent on top of that, totalling fifty per cent; in other words an original investment of £100 would become £150. In reality what the advertisement really meant was that investors would get market growth of ten per cent plus forty per cent of that, totalling fourteen per cent, so that an original investment of £100 would rise to £114. Of course the first interpretation was too good to be true, while the illustrations in the detailed description of the product were in line with the lower figure, so that more sophisticated investors would have had little trouble in interpreting the advertisement correctly, but many people with less understanding of reality did not.

Devotion to the whole truth can nevertheless sometimes go too far. Remember what happened to Gerald Ratner when he disarmingly told an audience at the annual meeting of the Institute of Directors in the Albert Hall that some of the jewellery he sold in his shops was 'crap'? The business did not survive long after that.

WASTE OF MONEY?

There are people, many of whom know little about business and even less about advertising, who are worried about how much advertising adds to the cost of heavily promoted products and the fact that competition is blamed for it. There are indeed cases of very high expenditure which have nothing whatever to do with the qualities of the product other than the need to distinguish it from its rivals.

In 1996 PepsiCo Inc turned its Pepsi branding to blue in order to distinguish itself from its main rival (Coca-Cola) and from lesser competitors. At a cost, alleged by journalist Joe Joseph of *The Times* to be £8 million, PepsiCo invited 500 journalists to Gatwick to see a Concorde airliner painted blue for the occasion and to meet three pop and sports stars. Apparently, in the words of their senior vice-president in charge of sales, the justification was that 'blue is modern and cool, exciting and dynamic and, most importantly, it's a colour that communicates refreshment'. He also said they believed that 'owning blue will give us a significant competitive advantage in the marketplace'. Joseph's article was less than complimentary, but PepsiCo still got forty-eight column inches in his paper alone. Four months later, PepsiCo had lost its chairman, who was supposed to be the mastermind of the campaign. Was it worth the $500 million which the *Financial Times* said it had cost?

The old adage of marketing people is that half the cost of advertising is wasted, but the difficulty is to know which half. One of the problems arising in this context especially, but not exclusively, with television and film advertising is whether the commercials are so sophisticated that the public remembers the advertisement but has no idea what the product is. To many people some of the posters that used to advertise various brands of cigarettes seemed obscure in the extreme and therefore a waste of money. In this case the trick was to engage the minds of the public and challenge them to recognize the brand – or at least the packaging.

Some of the most entertaining campaigns, such as the Nestlé soap opera about two well-heeled singles (which was even made into an indifferent novel), or the charming episodes featuring 'Papa' and 'Nicole' advertising a French car (which one?) achieved a cult status all of their own. Such campaigns establish a rapport with the public, which enjoys them for themselves. They can only be dismissed as a waste of money in advertising terms if they really fail in achieving that creation or maintenance of brand loyalty for which they are intended.

From both the business and the moral point of view it is important to make sure that advertising really is relevant and effective, so as to justify the cost that is eventually borne, primarily by consumers and shareholders.

THE NEW DIMENSION: THE INTERNET

The principles which have been the subject of the previous sections now need to be applied to a relatively new medium that is gaining importance at a tremendous speed, namely the Internet.

By its very nature, it is going to be very hard indeed to regulate advertising on the Internet because of both the difficulties of getting international agreement and the obstacles to enforcement. At the same time, the effectiveness of self-regulation is also extremely questionable, not least because the advertisers can now include not only those entities that have regulated themselves in traditional media (companies, advertising agencies, publishers and broadcasters), but also very small firms and individuals that are located anywhere in the world.

It may be difficult, but that is not a reason to sit back and do nothing. The International Chamber of Commerce (ICC) published its first attempt at a self-regulatory code in its *Guidelines on Interactive Marketing Communications* in 1998, sixty-one years after its first international advertising code. The

ICC believes that 'marketing and advertising on the Internet, the World Wide Web, and online services should reflect the highest standards of ethical conduct', as laid down in its existing codes. 'Responsible marketers and advertisers will therefore strive to create an electronic environment which all the world's consumers can fully trust.' This somewhat grandiose statement refers to the interest of business to enhance the confidence of the public in marketing through these interactive systems.

Apart from reiterating the principles of legality, honesty, decency and truthfulness, the *Guidelines* address a number of other key points, such as the need for advertisers to be clear in disclosing their identity, allowing individuals freedom not to receive commercial messages, clear statements about the costs of services offered, respect for data privacy and understanding the potential sensitivities of a global audience. Because interactive marketing and media were at such an early stage of development in 1996 when this piece of work on advertising practice was drawn up, the ICC has recognized the signs that the *Guidelines* would need frequent updating.

Competition to sell goods, services and information through the Internet and the Web is developing very rapidly and is already an attractive hunting ground for unprincipled operators. It would appear to be a matter of urgency for these imperfectly understood issues to be addressed by the international business community, both in its own interests and in those of the public. However, there can be no illusions about the limited effectiveness of the *Guidelines* or anything similar, and it would certainly be a dangerous delusion for consumers to think they have the same level of protection as is provided by conventional advertising codes. There are few areas where there is more need for ethical standards and, in their absence, *caveat emptor*.

CONCLUSION

Advertising is one of the essential tools for companies selling to the consumer, and to each other to a lesser extent. As with all other actions to achieve competitiveness, care must be taken to keep it within sensible bounds and to stick to the standards enshrined in its own codes. Individuals faced with ethical problems over advertising are fortunate in having such detailed support and guidance from these codes, which have been refined and revised over a long period and work well most of the time.

Even so, some people in advertising defend their own infringements of those standards by claiming they are only reflecting the values of those elements of the population at which their advertising is aimed. They consider it ridiculous to expect them to be moral guardians of the nation and believe that they have no social responsibility, though they often prefer to remain anonymous when they say so. Such people only do damage to the profession and the industry when they try to ride roughshod over the principles enshrined in codes, and risk the imposition of highly prescriptive curbs at the expense of well-tried and on the whole effective self-regulation.

The Advertising Association claims in its *Executive Briefs* that three-quarters of the population in the UK approves of advertising, while only about one-half does so in the US: 'The UK system of control is a world standard, and is frequently quoted as the most effective system ever developed.' It is important to keep it that way.

SOME ADVICE

The key points emerging from this chapter for individuals to think about in relation to advertising are as follows.

- Advertising and promotion, important as they are as essential competitive tools, need to be controlled if they are to be accepted by society.

- If advertising is to work effectively, it must be seen by those it seeks to influence to be honest, decent and credible.

- Advertisers should adhere both to the letter and the spirit of the self-regulatory codes that have been developed and improved for well over fifty years.

- If colleagues choose to ignore these codes, individuals must try to invoke the values and (where they exist) the general ethical codes of their company. Even if there is nothing specifically about advertising in these codes, there are usually general principles which can be applied and put into practice. Where there is no company code, then the individual can still resort to the utilitarian argument in favour of good practice, namely that advertising has to be credible and has to be trusted if it is to work.

- In the last resort, individuals may have to examine their own consciences in such matters.

There are few aspects of competition where there is better support from established best practice than in advertising. The very opposite is the case in relation to bribery, which is the subject of the next chapter.

Chapter 4

Bribery and entertaining

Some unethical practices adopted by business in order to gain an edge on competitors are discussed in Chapter 5. However, bribery and entertaining are classic examples of such practices, which raise most of the key questions relating to the ethics of competition and therefore merit a chapter to themselves.

Bribery is a highly complex problem because it is so widespread, varies so much in how it is carried out, involves such disparate parties and ranges from the passing of serious money into offshore bank accounts to seemingly trivial amounts or relatively modest benefits in kind. Because it is by its very nature secret, it is particularly difficult to combat effectively.

Business entertaining, which many people may be surprised to see lumped together with bribery, is much more visible and also varies in scale from lavish freebies in exotic locations to the continuation of a sales discussion over a pint in a pub. Such entertaining is so common and so widely accepted that attitudes to it are extremely varied. While bribery is clearly totally unethical, the issues relating to entertaining are both subjective and highly controversial.

In moral terms both givers and receivers of bribes and lavish entertainment are to blame, the latter being culpable of extortion, commercial blackmail or simple, small-scale venality. While recognizing that it takes two to tango, this chapter is concerned primarily with the giver because it is he or she who expects to obtain some competitive advantage as a result.

THE NATURE OF THE PROBLEM

Corruption is best defined as 'the misuse of public or corporate position or power for private gain'. When a company bribes a government official or someone in another company in order to obtain business, it is not only a deliberate distortion of fair competition on strictly commercial grounds but it also demeans the giver and undermines the receiver's position of trust.

The great paradox of corruption was expressed very simply by Professor Bruno Oppetit in an article in the Paris *Journal du Droit International*. He said it was unanimously disapproved of and universally prevalent. The level of disapproval could be non-existent or very low at the bottom end of the scale, but might be expected to increase higher up.

This is not always the case. It is normal for business people to ask their own country's overseas trade representatives for advice on the best agents to employ. It is far from unknown for the advice to take into account the agent's ability to influence the right people. Needless to say, the language used in such situations is prone to highly sophisticated euphemisms. George Moody-Stewart, in his book *Grand Corruption*, quotes with relish from the BBC-tv comedy series *Yes Minister*. In the episode entitled 'The Moral Dimension', the Minister, Jim Hacker, confronts his Permanent Secretary, the totally amoral Sir Humphrey Appleby, over condoning the use of bribery in winning an overseas contract. Sir Humphrey's memorable reply was: 'No, no, Minister, it could never be Government policy – that is unthinkable – only Government practice... this contract means thousands of British jobs, millions of export dollars. Surely you're not going to throw all that away because of some small technical irregularity?'

'Winning' contracts

When the *Yes Minister* writers, Antony Jay and Jonathan Lynn, wrote this episode, they probably had in mind big international contracts for dams, airports, roads or defence equipment in developing countries. Their fictional example is of the kind where the temptation (or the need, depending on where the individual stands in this matter) to bribe may be greatest. When a company or an individual is desperate for business, even when personal considerations such as bonuses or share options are excluded as motivation, it is only too easy to justify bribery on the grounds that the security of colleagues' jobs or the future of the company itself may depend on it.

One of the most famous cases was when Lockheed gave Japanese officials $12 million to get orders for Tristar aircraft in the 1970s. While admitting that both sides had acted unethically, Lockheed's defence was that there had been no violation of US legislation at that time and that the orders would benefit its stockholders, its employees and their dependants. Thus the benefits, it claimed, overrode moral considerations.

Too many companies justify bribery to themselves on the grounds that it is part of the culture ('when in Rome...'). This is a dangerous argument which can be self-confirming. The very assumption by a company from a developed country that a bribe is necessary to obtain a contract is a positive encouragement to the extortionists. Just because Nigeria, for example, has a terrible reputation for corruption, it does not mean that all Nigerians are corrupt or that they all condone the practice. Indeed one of the most outspoken critics of it is the former Head of State, General Obasanjo, who described this phenomenon in a speech at Entebbe in Uganda in 1994 in the following terms: '... it is simply a self-serving justification of reprehensible conduct for businessmen of the North... to claim that only by lavishly entertaining African leaders and educating their children can anyone do business on this continent.'

This shows that companies need to be sensitive to the reactions of countries generally regarded in the West as corrupt; there is always the danger of incurring counter-productive accusations of moral imperialism. Caterpillar recognizes this when it says in its own *Code of Ethics* that it does not want to force its own ethical standards on others or 'attempt to remake the world in the image of any one country or philosophy', but this does not stop it from having a tough code on corruption. Yet many companies fall back on the well known excuse that if they don't go along with bribery, another competitor (probably a *foreign* company) will. This is very often the case, resulting yet again in that well known demand for level playing fields.

One hard-learned lesson is that once companies become embroiled in bribery, it is quite hard to escape. One thing leads to another: for instance, a young salesman with a leading UK company, with very little overseas experience of his own, was keen to develop sales of one of the company's products by getting them specified by a public authority in a Near Eastern country. He was successful in doing this, thanks to the diligence of the local agent in providing lavish entertainment and other inducements to representatives of the authority concerned. He flew out to see them in the hope of securing yet more business, without knowing that his valued customers had been found out and put in jail for corruption. It was, therefore, a nasty surprise when he was arrested on arrival. His employers at home were concerned about conditions in that country's prisons and therefore asked the police to bail him and, while retaining his passport, to hold him instead in a hotel where he would at least have access to bottled water. This was duly arranged, but only after the company had paid a suitable 're-imbursement' to the police for their trouble.

It is far easier for companies to forego business when the potential is not very great. In the 1950s a young steel salesman from a small company, hungry for orders after the end of post-war shortages, visited a buyer to try to get an order for steel pit props for coalmines. The buyer was friendly and the prospect looked promising. Towards the end of the meeting the salesman was handed a card with the buyer's home address on the back. He thanked the buyer politely and sought orders elsewhere. No doubt the buyer got the pit props he needed and maybe also a case of whisky delivered to his home. In this example, the salesman 'did the right thing'; the question is whether he would have been able to resist the temptation had the potential order been much bigger and the commission earned significant to his obtaining a mortgage or taking a special holiday.

Petty corruption

Another aspect of bribery can be described loosely as administrative – to get things done that ought to be done anyway, often by people who are already paid to do so. This form of corruption (or 'grease', as it is often called) seems harmless enough to otherwise honest individuals, especially at the moment of need. A small bribe to get a telephone installed quickly even in some developed countries or the 'dash' to guarantee a seat on an internal flight in West Africa, can usually be justified because of the often trivial amounts involved and the convenience so achieved. Moreover, such practices are regarded in many countries as essential to keep the wheels turning in the local economy and a necessary addition to the income of the underpaid officials, who are responsible for the extortion in the first place.

At first sight, this type of corruption may not appear to have much to do with competition for contracts, but once an individual or company starts on the slippery slope, any such distinction can become blurred. Likewise, much petty corruption is carried out by individuals not for their personal benefit but in their capacity as employees of companies. There are obvious problems when the company itself becomes involved or the sums involved are more significant. A simple example of the former relates to a foreign company in Milan that needed to install its first computer as a matter of urgency but had no space in the office for the bulky equipment needed in the 1960s (to do work which today could be done on a PC). A small building was rented nearby and a lot of money was spent converting its interior. The computer was duly installed before planning permission, believed to be a mere formality, had been received. Six months later, permission had still not come in, and the consequences of refusal in operational, and therefore competitive, terms were by then very serious. The solution involved handing over a bundle of notes on a street corner, not to bend the planning rules, but merely to get the relevant document into the functionary's out-tray. The sum involved was small enough to be easily 'lost' in the accounts. At the time and in the circumstances, this seemed sensible to those responsible (especially as the head office back home did not know about it), but of course it was unethical.

A more serious example involved a large multinational company operating in a country in South America. The company employed a small number of expatriates in its senior positions. Finding that the managing director's work permit had expired and realizing that there could be considerable inconvenience if it were not renewed quickly, the finance director enquired how long it would take. He was informed that a speedy renewal could indeed be arranged, but only at a cost. He unwisely decided to accede to the demand, even though it was explicitly forbidden in company rules. His action came to the knowledge of his head office, and both he and the MD were sacked.

Morally, there is not much difference between the two examples, but in practical terms the main difference lies in the fact that the perpetrator in the first case was not found out. This is one of the reasons why it is so hard to combat the problem.

In the former Soviet command economy, petty corruption was widespread because there were endemic shortages of supply due to the absence of competition and the inefficiency of the distribution system. Bribes were offered to suppliers of scarce products and gratefully accepted, the justification being the benefits to the receiving factory and its customers, who might have to pay further bribes themselves. Needless to say, the scale of such corruption could be anything but petty, resulting in serious distortions to the economy. In the satellite countries of Eastern Europe, corrupt practices were often justified as a patriotic way of defying the central oppressor and then became entrenched, while in Russia itself its old habits are dying hard. This is an even greater problem where employees are not paid at all for months on end.

Moral and practical consequences

The circumstances described above show what some of the consequences of bribery are. They can be summarized as follows:

- it creates false relationships between the parties concerned;

- by its very nature it is hidden and thus an enemy of transparency and accountability;

- it increases the cost of doing business;

- it is inefficient because it can divert tenders away from the most suitable supplier and thus distort the correct allocation of resources;

- in undermining honest business, it can act as a discouragement to legitimate trade and investment;

- experience shows it can damage the quality of overseas aid programmes by inflating the cost of projects and diverting funds from more deserving ones;

- the cash flows involved usually evade taxation and often require money laundering, involving links with other forms of international commercial crime;

- once started, escape is very difficult (payment of Danegeld did not stop the Danes coming!);

■ it demeans the individuals involved in it, breeds cynicism and destroys trust;

■ it is a moral and financial gangrene that contributes to a general corruption of standards in business and public life and, by association, damages free market ideals;

■ on a grand scale (eg in some Eastern European, Middle Eastern, Asian, South American and African countries) it can become a moral threat to society in general and to democracy in particular.

LEGAL PROBLEMS IN OVERCOMING BRIBERY

The toughest legislation prohibiting bribery is the Foreign Corrupt Practices Act (FCPA) introduced by the United States in 1977, which is distinguished by being applicable extra-territorially as well as at home. It is notable that this Act legitimized the minor administrative forms of bribery described above. This could be deemed sensible pragmatism or a flaw, depending on one's point of view.

The whole question is a legal minefield. However much general agreement there may be among responsible business people and lawyers about the evils of bribery, there is far less agreement on how to overcome the very complex and practical problems in countering it. Indeed, there is a view that some harm is being done by the campaigners in their pushing for ill-considered action to be taken, and an apparent lack of understanding on the part of those trying to draw up workable regulations.

One of the great difficulties is to achieve uniform legislation, uniformly enforced, in large numbers of countries, which is very necessary because of the international nature of so much bribery. Such an approach has long been sought by the US in the interests of fair competition. However, twenty years after the passing of the FCPA some countries still tolerate the practice of bribery by excluding it from their criminal law; indeed, it can be argued that countries where it is allowable for tax purposes positively encourage it.

Many countries prohibit bribery at home, but until recently applied this prohibition little or not at all to actions wholly undertaken abroad. This allows otherwise honest people to justify their actions because they are not illegal. Moreover, few of them are involved personally: most bribes are not paid directly by the companies involved but by agents using part of their commission for the purpose, so that the bribe is hidden in the accounts as part of the cost of sales. Enforcement of any suitable legislation, whatever its nature, is always very difficult because of the secrecy involved and because so much of the evidence is anecdotal.

Even US-based companies, desperate for business, have been known to take the risk of being found out. George Moody-Stewart, in *Grand Corruption*, relates how an African acquaintance once described a particularly crude instance of bribery by a US company as having been perpetrated by 'an outfit which gives corruption a bad name'.

One way in which the problem can be tackled effectively through the law is for there to be a uniform approach between countries to the criminalization of bribery, the elimination of tax deductibility and international cross-frontier co-operation in enforcement. This includes the principle of *chercher l'argent* – concentrated efforts to trace laundered funds, much of which may have been generated by other forms of crime.

THE ROLE OF BUSINESS

While there is an absence of universal, effective, enforced legislation, it is important for business to try to tackle the problem through self-regulation, thus reducing it at source. Some readers with direct experience of the reality of corruption will smile at the idealism of trying to create a situation where no competitors give in to extortion, but ethically this must be addressed.

The idea is not new. The first co-ordinated international attempt to deal with bribery followed the previously mentioned Lockheed scandal in the 1970s. The Paris-based International Chamber of Commerce (ICC), with members in both developed and developing countries, set up a working group under Britain's Lord Shawcross to prepare a statement comprising a code of practice for business and recommendations on action for governments – *Extortion and Bribery in Business Transactions*, published in 1977. This document suggested what governments should do to strengthen the law and make enforcement effective, and also urged the drafting of an international treaty sponsored by the United Nations. The brief code for business included the point that agents' commissions should be no more than appropriate remuneration for their services and that principals should specifically require the agent to agree to the code.

All this was fine in theory, but could it be made to stick? The ICC's document provided for the setting up of a panel to oversee and review the code and consider alleged infringements. A good try, but it just did not work in practice, because companies were not prepared to sit in judgment on their peers. Some twenty years later, the ICC began working on a revision to the code, which was published in 1996. The new document repeated clauses in the original 1977 version, but strengthened it in several respects. The 1977 rules only prohibited extortion and bribery in connection with obtaining and retaining business; the new version prohibits such activities for any purpose, for example the influencing of judicial proceedings, tax questions, and environmental or other regulatory matters. The ICC undertook to promote this code, but this time round did not make the mistake of implying it could enforce it.

The ICC's original seed-sowing did not entirely fall on stony ground. In the years that followed, more and more European companies included clauses prohibiting bribery in their own codes of conduct. For example, the Institute of Business Ethics (IBE), from its foundation in the UK in 1986, included anti-bribery clauses in its model codes and encouraged companies to include them in theirs. Its 1993 'Illustrative Code', forming a chapter within its *Code of Business Ethics* written by Simon Webley, read as follows: 'No employee may give money or any gift of significant value to a customer. Nor may any gift or service be given which could be construed as being intended as a bribe.'

In drawing up this recommendation, Webley drew freely on existing best practice, especially from US companies working under the constraints imposed by the FCPA. Caterpillar, for example, is blunt and to the point: 'We won't seek to influence sales of our products (or other events impacting on the company) by payments of bribes, kickbacks, or other questionable inducements.' On the question of small 'tips' for administrative services (eg getting visas quickly), they are rather more flexible in saying that where 'unavoidable, they must be limited to customary amounts'.

Some companies make it clear that they see little distinction between bribery and other inducements, which are dealt with later in this chapter. A good example is from the code of conduct of another leading US company, Du Pont – a company that '... does not seek to gain any advantage through the improper use of business courtesies or any other inducements. Good judgment and moderation must be exercised to avoid misinterpretation and adverse effect on the reputation of the Company or its employees. Offering, giving, soliciting or receiving of any form of bribe is prohibited.' The code goes on to say: 'Gifts, favors and entertainment may be given if they:

- are consistent with customary business practices

- are not excessive in value and cannot be considered as a bribe or pay-off

- are not in contravention of applicable law or ethical standards

- will not embarrass the Company or the employee if publicly disclosed.'

Notable here is the requirement for moderation and the need to avoid harm to the company. Du Pont is very tough on the receiving of bribes or inducements from its suppliers, but when it comes to selling, it is careful to distinguish in its codes of practice between legitimate commissions and the giving or receiving of individual inducements: 'Such business-inducement payments must be reasonable in value, competitively justified, properly documented and made to the business entity to whom the original sales agreement or invoice was made/issued. They should not be made to individual officers, employees or agents of such entity or to a related business entity...' There seems to be some flexibility over bribes of an administrative nature: 'Although discouraged, "facilitating" payments are permitted if they are legal, necessary, follow an established well-recognised practice in the area, and are for administrative actions to which the Company is clearly entitled. These payments should be properly approved and recorded.'

This policy is a reflection of the specific legal constraints on US companies, which of course reach out to associates or subsidiaries elsewhere. For example, Rank Xerox required any attempt at extortion to be turned down. Any alternative course of action was to be reported with recommendations to the MD of Rank Xerox Ltd, who was then required to consult the President of Xerox Corporation.

UK companies tend to go into less detail, but the principles of transparency and the preservation of the reputation of the company are similar. For example, British Aerospace lays down that 'it is essential that all such agency and consultancy arrangements are properly regulated and recorded and that they conform with normally-accepted business practices'. Explaining that more detailed procedures are issued from time to time, BAe says that 'under no circumstances will the Board of the Company countenance corrupt practices, including payments or other inducements being given by employees to political parties, government officials or a customer's executives...' With similar sentiment, Standard Chartered Bank is brief and to the point: it states that 'nothing may be given or received which might distort commercial judgment or harm the group's reputation.'

Ten years after the IBE started work, just about half of the '*Times* 500' (ie the top 500 firms in the UK) had brought out written codes, the vast majority of which included articles on the giving and receiving of gifts, thus covering entertaining as well. However, including the renunciation of bribery in codes is of course not enough. There can unfortunately be a world of difference between what some companies say they do in theory and what happens in the hard real world where the pressures of competition are severe. In his book *Grand Corruption*, George Moody-Stewart classifies companies into three groups:

■ those that are 'either so strong or unchallenged in their own field that they are immune to all pressures';

■ those that, for one reason or another, do not know what is being done in their name or on their behalf;

■ those that are 'simply lying'.

Moody-Stewart quotes the managing director of a company in the first group whom he knew very well as saying that he was 'very lucky to work for a company which is strong enough never to have to pay a bribe. We can afford, if necessary, to walk away from a major contract.' As far as the other two categories are concerned, it is obvious that the remedy must be:

- effective promulgation of the code or statement of principles to all relevant members of management;

- management systems, including internal auditors, to ensure compliance;

- regular reporting to the company's Board on the above.

Even this, as has been explained, is not necessarily enough, but it does show the company takes the issue seriously. A good example of best practice is the leading international mining group RTZ, now Rio Tinto, which requires employees to sign declarations of conformity as part of their personal annual assessments and includes a declaration to that effect in its internal reporting procedures.

In spite of the fact that progress is being made by the larger, more reputable companies, especially those that are US-owned because of the severity of their legislation, there are continual breaches of codes (especially, everyone smugly thinks, by rivals in other countries, no matter which nationality is speaking) while there are still many that have no codes of practice at all. It is claimed by some that corruption of this kind is on the increase. One person who takes this view is Peter Eigen, a German who set up a non-profit-making, non-governmental organization (NGO) called Transparency International (TI), which works internationally to encourage governments and inter-governmental organizations (IGOs) to tackle the problem of bribery and corruption through effectively implemented laws and international conventions. It seeks to strengthen public support and understanding in order to pressurize both business and governments to do better, and it has set up 'chapters' in many countries including, significantly, several in Eastern Europe.

TI has no illusions that the task is easy or that effective solutions will be achieved quickly. It realizes that the problem has to be addressed in many different ways, and as part of the process it has contributed to the revision of the ICC Code, recognizing that the world's leading business organization with members in developed and developing countries can be influential in bringing about change. Both TI and the ICC want to see the business world make a real effort to reduce bribery before effective international regulations can be agreed. The onus is primarily on companies themselves, but it is necessary for other professional and industrial bodies to play their part.

One such initiative came from the International Federation of Consulting Engineers (FIDIC). In the knowledge that companies and consulting engineers involved in international construction contracts are subject to particular pressures from extortionists, it issued in 1996 a Policy Statement on corruption which said that 'the consulting engineering industry, which has historically been, as it should be, motivated by the needs of society, must seek both to prevent and react to the blight of corruption. FIDIC and its member associations, representing the leaders of the consulting engineering industry, will neither ignore nor acquiesce with the tide of corruption, nor will it consider that local corruption is cultural and unchangeable. The member firms of FIDIC's Member Associations will neither initiate nor accede to corrupt practices.' The Policy Statement included seven recommendations, one of which was notable for its requirement that there should be disciplinary action against member firms found to have violated the FIDIC code, including expulsion from the national organization and the reporting of any such breach to the 'public authorities'. Some of the introductory paragraphs and the recommendations are reproduced herein as Appendix B.

All the business organizations mentioned in this chapter recognize that there is no chance of solving the problem on their own, however much they may prefer self-regulation. As is discussed later in Chapter 6, effective regulation can be the best way of achieving a level playing field. As with other business issues, it follows that success depends on the closest possible collaboration of business with governments and IGOs.

THE ROLE OF INTER-GOVERNMENTAL ORGANIZATIONS

The idea of an international convention on bribery with realistic and effective powers has always been attractive. In the 1980s and most of the 1990s there have been, in the words of François Vincke, Secretary General of Petrofina of Belgium, 'declarations of intent deprived of any operational value'. Vincke, who chairs the ICC's working party on this question, was thinking of IGOs but, as has already been suggested above, the same criticism can be levelled at some sections of the business community. In practice, all the parties involved – business, IGOs and governments – need the mutual encouragement that is to be derived from each other's actions.

Work by the OECD

The ICC believes that its 1977 initiative helped (if only too slowly) the Organization for Economic Co-operation and Development (OECD) to get its own Recommendation off the ground in 1994. This Recommendation covered the necessary points and was in theory an important step forward, but because it was non-binding it was toothless until all the signatories, which are developed countries, were prepared to act upon it. Furthermore, any international convention on this subject must eventually include developing countries as well, and above all every country where there is a particular problem. Achieving an effective agreement among over 190 nations is a daunting and distant prospect; all that can be hoped for is a step-by-step approach, with the developed countries taking the lead.

By 1996 the OECD Council of Ministers approved a second Recommendation that those member countries that allowed tax deductibility of bribes paid to foreign public officials should re-examine their laws on the matter. In 1997 the Council, which by now represented 29 developed countries, formalized it into a Convention, binding 'member countries [to] criminalize the bribery of foreign public officials in an effective and co-ordinated manner by submitting proposals to their legislative bodies by 1 April 1998... and seeking their enactment by the end of 1998'.

This is the first time the OECD has sought to enact a binding Convention on business and it may seem to be an important step forward. It was welcomed especially by the US government and business community because of the competitive disadvantage imposed on them by the Foreign Corrupt Practices Act. The question arises to what extent, in the short term, it will prove to be workable. An article in the *International Herald Tribune* summed this up by saying that 'it will be a long time, if ever, before the champagne is poured'.

Many people in industry do not disguise their reservations about the OECD's move, because the Convention was drafted by people with little understanding of its practical implications. This is not the place to go into the legal arguments, but suffice it to say that it contains no provisions to deal with extortion and that, because it is legally defective, accountants and lawyers would have a field day advising companies on its implications.

The Council of Europe and the EU

The Council of Europe (CoE) performs work in the same area as the OECD, work which stemmed from its conditions of membership, including the maintenance of genuine democracy, the rule of law and the upholding of human rights. Conventions already exist on extradition and money laundering, and a Convention on bribery is under consideration.

The multi-disciplinary group set up to produce such a Convention, which included the CoE's own members, some other OECD countries, nine African countries and representatives of other IGOs including the EU, the European Bank for Reconstruction and Development (EBRD) and the OECD itself, has moved very slowly towards producing model laws, codes of conduct and follow-up mechanisms that would complement the OECD's work in this area. How effective this Convention will be in getting broadly similar legislation through on a tight timetable is an open question.

Meanwhile the European Union (EU) itself already has binding provisions in place in respect of conduct that would damage its financial resources. There is also advanced work in applying these principles outside the EU. This is important because the EU is a powerful, manageable and cohesive group of countries that make up over half the membership of the OECD.

Other IGOs

Other IGOs which can play a useful part in the fight to reduce corruption are the World Trade Organization (WTO), the World Bank and the International Monetary Fund (IMF). Because bribery is an obvious threat to competition in international trade, it is becoming an issue for consideration by the WTO. At its 1996 ministerial conference in Singapore, it agreed to establish a working group to study questions related to public procurement. Whether this will develop into more than a talking shop remains to be seen.

The World Bank and the IMF are in a strong position to exercise real leverage because they are concerned with lending to governments. There is nothing like the threat of the suspension of a loan to concentrate the mind of a corrupt government. In mid 1997, the IMF issued guidelines on the subject with a view to assisting economic progress and fostering more confidence in the private sector of business by reducing corrupt practices in client countries.

The simple lesson from all of this is that there is no single solution to a very complex ethical problem. The IGOs can only achieve anything with the willing co-operation of their member governments and they in turn can only achieve anything with the active participation of business and public opinion generally. Meanwhile the cocktail of Conventions and laws emerging from all these acting bodies, however worthy the objective, presents business people, who above all want to know where they stand in such matters, with formidable challenges – and their professional advisers with plenty of work.

THE ETHICS OF BUSINESS ENTERTAINING

So many people benefit personally from business entertaining, whether as providers or receivers, that most of them would be outraged at the suggestion that it was in any way a harmful, if indirect, form of bribery. In excess, such expenditure is considered obscene by the critics of business. These attitudes are undoubtedly in many cases fuelled by envy, as many of those same critics appear only too ready to benefit should the opportunity come their way. Moreover, ostentatious freebies never were the sole privilege of business, as MPs, local government officials and many others have shown often enough.

Apart from anything else, there are some very considerable untaxed benefits involved. The Inland Revenue and similar government authorities would like to get their hands on more of this if the administrative costs of doing so were not so high.

Practical considerations

High-profile and expensive entertaining, whether at big sporting events, Glyndebourne or smart Caribbean resorts, is justified by many as a way of building personal relationships outside the normal business environment, of rewarding good customers or persuading others to buy. As beneficiaries themselves, the organizers are less inhibited by moral concerns than by whether the entertainment is cost-effective.

Some companies sponsoring sporting events find that too many of their salespeople spend more time with each other than with clients, while some of the latter, so used to being asked to such occasions, have been known not to remember who their host was. Many clients are not the slightest bit interested in the sport in question, being more drawn to the bar than to what is going on outside, while guests at a modern opera at Glyndebourne have been heard to say that they were surprised Mozart sounded like that.

'So what?' will be the aggrieved reaction of many readers. They will be the first to reject the argument that such entertaining may not always be effective, appropriate or necessary. Yet two simple examples from past experience may help illustrate the point. First, a junior employee at a multinational's head office in London was asked by his boss, because he spoke German, to entertain an important non-English-speaking customer and his wife from near Stuttgart. They were to be offered anything they liked – theatre, smart restaurant, nightclub: no expense was to be spared. It had to be good because the customer had just come from the US, where he had been fêted lavishly by some of the company's main competitors. The young man did as he was bidden but also offered them an alternative: would they like to have supper with him and his wife (who also spoke German) in their tiny house where there was food in stock and a six-month-old baby as well. They accepted enthusiastically – he with relief, after weeks in American hotels. Next morning the young man put in for his expenses – a trifling sum for a bottle of wine – and was torn off a strip for disobeying orders. In contrast to the boss's fury, the company's sales director in Germany reported that the London visit had been the highlight of his customer's whole trip, and he and his wife became lifelong friends of the young couple.

The second example is from Yorkshire. The export manager of a medium-sized company, a man of high personal ethical standards, had to entertain an important customer from the Middle East. Knowing the predilection of some such gentlemen for fleshpots and knowing Leeds had some to offer, he very tentatively suggested that the visitor might like to see the bluebells in full bloom in a wood in Wharfedale instead and have a meal at a country restaurant afterwards. The customer accepted the offer and never forgot the experience.

Company policies on entertaining

There is evidence of a change in corporate culture with regard to entertaining, driven undoubtedly by considerations of cost-effectiveness, especially in times of recession, but also by some moral considerations.

As has already been indicated above, there is an increasing tendency for company codes of conduct to cover all forms of bribery and entertaining, with strict clauses on the giving and receiving of all such inducements. Interestingly, codes tend to be much tougher and more specific on the *receiving* of such entertainment, in an attempt to ensure the incorruptibility of purchasing staff, than on the *giving,* where there seems to be less inhibition in trying to influence customers through such means. One of the best statements on the principles applying both to receiving and giving comes from Esso UK:

> The company's business interests are best served when its relationships are based on commercial criteria and not influenced by such factors as gifts or entertainment. In this way, the Company is able to sustain constructive, ongoing relationships with those organisations, firms and individuals doing business or seeking to do business with it... Accordingly, the extension of non-cash gifts, meals, entertainment, travel, and other favours to business contacts or by such contacts to Company employees should be moderate, infrequent, appropriate to the occasion, and in accordance with our ethics and conflicts of interest policies.

The key points generally covered in such codes are moderation, transparency and reciprocity. On the question of moderation, House of Fraser simply says that 'excessive entertainment of any sort is not acceptable'. ICI says that entertainment should only be offered 'consistent with customary business practice, modest in value and not in contravention of any applicable law'. Esso UK says that 'employees should not give or receive extravagant entertainment, including free airline tickets, hotel accommodation not strictly necessary for business purposes, or free use of expensive recreational facilities'. Blue Circle says that 'the gift or entertainment (made or received) should not be of such value as to constitute an unusual personal enrichment for the recipient'. Dixons, with similar standards, says that senior executives must lead by example and that 'when in doubt, don't go out'.

On the matter of transparency, Whitbread, after saying that 'common courtesies... should be reasonable and justifiable', requires that 'records should be kept by each employee to demonstrate that the amounts accepted meet the [company's] criteria'. And on reciprocity, British Gas says: 'Business entertainment should be on a reciprocal basis' and Thorn EMI (as it used to be) said the same for entertainment by/for its procurement staff.

It will be seen that there is a great deal of room for flexibility in the way in which all these codes on entertainment can be interpreted, followed and monitored. Some cynics would say they mean very little, though greater stringency is to be expected on a company's own purchasing staff than on its salespeople.

One company, The John Lewis Partnership, has a deserved reputation for very high standards in such matters. There is detailed information about the Partnership and its values at Appendix C. Their Rules governing gifts and hospitality are reproduced at Appendix D. Because of the nature of the Partnership, the employees (ie the Partners), who have a direct personal interest, are the first to challenge the extent to which the Rules are followed, especially by the Partners at the top. Twenty years ago, this was less likely to happen.

In the vast majority of companies at that time, the propriety of giving and receiving such hospitality would not have been questioned and the John Lewis Rules would have been considered unnecessarily restrictive in this context. Twenty years later most people would probably take the same view. But as the case study at Appendix D shows, John Lewis Partners, acting either from high principles or from malice or envy, are only too willing to exercise their right to question such matters through letters to the John Lewis *Gazette*. Usually such letters are anonymous, but they are still answered by management who clearly, but understandably, find some of the points raised quite hard to handle, because the Rules do not explicitly cover every complex, or even simple, situation.

As will be seen later in Chapter 6, the higher the standards a company is seen to have, the more open to criticism it can become from its own staff or from outside. Whatever those standards may be, whether they are formalized codes or not, the attitude to accepting hospitality depends on the standards set at the top and on whether or not they are followed rigorously in a company. Once again, it is often a matter of individual conscience whether entertaining or being entertained is justified and at what level.

In response to various scandals including the alleged passing of brown envelopes to public servants and entertaining in expensive Paris hotels, and to the publication of a report by a committee chaired by Lord Nolan, a booklet entitled *Negotiating Nolan – a Guide to Business Ethics in the Public Sector* was written in 1997 by Dr Michael Harte, a former senior civil servant in the Ministry of Defence, to lay down ground rules for public servants. It recommended that offers of hospitality worth more than £100 should be declined, thus cutting out decent seats at Wimbledon, Covent Garden or Glyndebourne. Dr Harte's booklet also bans overnight stays, free transport (except from the nearest station or airport), and any gift worth more than £50. The message is, of course, also directed at business. In practice, different government departments have different sets of rules for their officials, but publications of this sort complement those of companies that might otherwise think they can achieve a measure of competitiveness on the back of human frailty.

CONCLUSION AND ADVICE

It is quite obvious from the preceding sections on bribery and business entertaining that there are no simple solutions to highly complex – and controversial – moral problems.

Bribery is condoned by a silent, shoulder-shrugging majority. Yet there is no more justification for cynical doubt as to whether the problem can be solved than there is for a naïve belief that somehow human goodness will prevail. It is also naïve to expect rapid elimination of the problem from countries where bribery is endemic. Only collective effort will count in the end, the need being for action at all levels of government and business, and across frontiers, in order to deal with the problem through the law, through voluntary codes and through the exercise of conscience. The only way to proceed is incrementally, creating what have been most aptly called 'islands of integrity' from which these forms of corruption will be driven.

Action by companies

In this context the responsibilities of companies are threefold. They should:

1. contribute by their actions and policies to the collective effort to overcome bribery, which is not only wrong in itself but distorts competition;

2. ensure that actions taken in their name or on their behalf avoid damage or discredit to themselves;

3. avoid putting their employees in impossible situations.

In order to achieve all three of these objectives, directors and senior managers need to lead by example to demonstrate their own integrity. They also need to establish clear policies on the issues and promulgate those policies to all who need to know them. Managements must ensure that anyone representing their company is fully briefed on what pressures may be expected and what actions they may or may not take. Whether company policies are included in written codes of practice or disseminated by other means, there should be procedures to monitor that they are effective. It is also advisable to establish 'hot lines' so that people at any level can appeal for advice independent of their own chain of command on what they should do when faced by extortionists.

The more that companies do in these ways, the better.

Actions by individuals

What advice do individuals need when faced with hard decisions in this context? 'Islands of integrity' can indeed be lonely places. People who try to take a stand alone against all the pressures may be morally justified and may make their contribution to the reduction of corrupt practices, but in the meantime vital business can be lost to competitors with fewer moral scruples and the individuals' own careers jeopardized. Individuals must therefore:

- make sure they are adequately briefed by their company on these matters in advance of being faced with difficult situations;

- check, where such advanced advice has not been given, on the legal position, which is especially important as the law is being progressively tightened up in many countries;

- check whether what they are being asked to do conforms with stated company policy;

- check actual and potential action against any professional codes external to the company that may be applicable;

- consult superiors or an independent source of advice or 'hot line';

- in the last analysis, consult their own consciences and the possible consequences of either standing on principle or not doing so.

As regards entertaining, no two people will agree where the line should be drawn between legitimate hospitality and excessive inducements. As has been seen, many companies have themselves tried to produce guidelines, most of which are open to fairly broad interpretation.

A loyal employee (rather than one who is cynical and self-serving) will follow company rules and, where those are either non-existent or just not helpful, will decide whether offering hospitality is appropriate from the company's point of view in the circumstances. When, in such instances, individuals find themselves on their own, they can only be guided by a subtle combination of their own principles, the size of their budgets and the venality of the people being entertained.

Chapter 5

Bringing the company into disrepute?

The list of unethical business practices that can be adopted (and even justified by some) for competitive reasons could be very long. In this chapter a few have been selected as being more closely related to competition as such, rather than to business in general. Such practices vary greatly in degree and in their impropriety in the eye of the beholder, depending on individuals' ideas of right and wrong. There are many grey areas, ranging from downright deliberate wrongdoing to instances of moral turpitude. In most instances they do, however, exclude actions prohibited by law, the most extreme of which would be to murder a competitor – an option (as much as one might sometimes want to) best left to drug dealers and *mafiosi*.

The unethical business practices to be considered in this chapter relate to five different aspects of business:

1. *Products*, including copying, counterfeiting and selling inappropriate products;

2. *Pricing policies*, including pricing what the market will bear, 'double pricing', 'loss leaders' and predatory pricing;

3. *Purchasing*, focusing on the exercise of excessive purchasing power in various ways rather than on corrupt practices (which have already been covered in the previous chapter);

4. *People*, concerning the treatment of employees, the closely linked question of excessive pay of people at the top of organizations, pay and benefit differentials between the financial centres and manufacturing industry, and poaching trained staff;

5. *Industrial espionage and intelligence*, which is self-explanatory.

The common feature of all of these practices is that they bring both the perpetrators and competition itself into disrepute.

PRODUCTS

Copying and counterfeiting

Competitive aspects of patent and trade mark protection were touched on briefly in Chapter 2.

One of the typical ethical 'grey areas' is where products are presented in such a way that they look like their better-known rivals. Familiar examples of supermarket look-alike own brands are plain chocolate, breakfast cereals and cola. Tesco, as the leading UK supermarket chain, promised in 1997 to stop such packaging and to promote its own-brand products more strongly.

Companies and their employees can come up against hard decisions as to whether such practices are fair competition or unethical. This often depends in turn on who is the judge – the copier, the copied or the consumer. Coca-Cola became so concerned about this that they successfully challenged supermarkets on this practice, while McDonald's fights hard to avoid near-copies of their logo at other burger bars.

Decisions are sometimes taken to adopt misleading packaging more out of poor judgment than lack of ethics, as illustrated by this 1997 case involving a highly reputable company. Cadbury introduced into the UK a new product, which they had already sold in Australia, a 'Honey-flavour Milk Chocolate with Pieces of Almond Nougat'. There was nothing wrong with the product itself, but it was packaged as 'Cadbury's Swiss Chalet' with an unmistakable image of the Matterhorn in the background. The Swiss chocolate industry adopted a similar line to French champagne producers in their own dispute with near-copiers, namely that the public would be misled into thinking that the product was genuinely Swiss, and they took Cadbury to court. A British High Court judge took the view that some consumers would be so misled, rejected Cadbury's argument that quite a lot of chocolate sold under Swiss brands was made in other countries, and ruled in favour of the plaintiffs. The product in this packaging had to be withdrawn from the market.

Product counterfeiting is a different matter altogether. It is theft. Counterfeiters are criminals. They defraud brand owners and bring them into disrepute with their poor-quality copies. But consumers are willingly and often knowingly accessories to their crimes; many who have bought such products, from 'Lacoste' shirts to 'Rolex' watches, boast about the 'bargains' they picked up in

Singapore or Bangkok and justify their actions by saying that the makers of luxury branded luggage or perfume deserve the competition they get from counterfeiters. If, after buying fake Chanel on a street stall, they find they smell like a goat – then tough: *caveat emptor.*

In Eastern Europe, where branding was virtually unknown under Communism, consumers considered logos on their jeans and shirts to be purely decorative, not understanding at all that product differentiation was essential to achieving competition and consumer choice. Sometimes fake products are just amusingly absurd: Eric Ellen, head of the London-based International Counterfeiting Intelligence Bureau, once found a 'scotch' whisky in India which claimed it was:

Genuine Scotch Whisky
Brewed from real Scottish Grapes
Matured in the Cellars of Buckingham Palace

The practice is anything but a joke when safety is involved, as was the case when a truck with counterfeit brake linings lost control and killed people at the bottom of a hill. The risk can be even more serious when the spare parts are fitted on a helicopter, or when fake ingredients are used to make medicinal products. For example, a World Health Organization report in 1992 deplored the frightening proportion of fake pharmaceuticals sold in some African countries: in one hospital in Nigeria, around a hundred children died after being given paracetamol made from counterfeit chemicals.

Counterfeiting can not only endanger consumers in these ways and take legitimate business from the producers of the genuine product, it can also have wider effects. Anthea Worsdell, of the UK Anti-Counterfeiting Group, points out that a purchaser of a $30 counterfeit 'Rolex', who would never have been able to afford the real thing, is then unlikely to buy a genuine $30 Swatch. In other words, the damage is far wider than to the original owner of the brand. Counterfeiters are part of the black economy, ignoring employment protection law and of course evading taxes.

Breaches of copyright protection raise similar issues, which are very serious for the original owners. It is absolutely ethical for an author of a book, a musician whose work is on a compact disc, or the developer of software to be protected. But such protection is notoriously difficult to enforce on a world scale. Publishers of medical textbooks lose vast amounts of money because their products are pirated in third-world countries, while the copiers try to justify their actions on grounds of need.

Two of the biggest problem areas here are compact discs and computer software. As regards the former, in some countries consumers feel justified in buying counterfeit compact discs on the grounds (which are to some extent correct) that the products are overpriced. There is a particular problem in countries where enforcement is weak – for example, in 1996 it was alleged by the industry that in Hungary there were twenty counterfeits for every legitimate CD sold. As regards the latter, it is well known that individual consumers are not the only ones at fault, for companies also find it only too easy to save money by acquiring pirated copies of computer software. Even high-principled companies were quite slow to recognize this and as a result forbid the practice in their own codes – as late as 1993, the Institute of Business Ethics did not mention the avoidance of software piracy in its recommended model codes.

Individual consumers, by buying cheap counterfeits, are far from unwilling accessories to this criminal activity, partly because copying is so easy in the case of software. And laws in different countries to deal with counterfeiting and copyright infringement are uneven to say the least, while enforcement across frontiers is notoriously difficult. Consumers who collude with the practice of counterfeiting do not realize the extent to which it is a threat to fair and legitimate competition; nor do they realize that the easy pickings in this area have attracted organized crime.

In conclusion on this topic, it has to be said that all counterfeiting and copyright piracy is both morally unacceptable and illegal, and so the obvious advice to companies and individuals is quite simply 'don't do it'. Readers may be affronted by the idea they could ever be so involved, but they may well have been unwittingly on the other side of the transaction. Is their company meticulous in buying software and not copying it from others? Are they, as private individuals, sure that they do not condone the practice by buying counterfeit or pirated products?

Product look-alikes are a different matter. As has been said, it is up to companies to set their own standards on the extent to which they want their products to look like those of leading competitors, even if thereby there is no infraction of the trade-mark rights of the latter. The principle, whether enshrined in company codes or not, must surely be that any product should sell on its own merits and should be marketed accordingly. Enthusiastic members of the marketing function should think about this, even take advice from legal colleagues, before such products are brought into the range.

Selling inappropriate products

This is a vast subject covering products that are known to carry dangers to users or to the environment, and products that are thought not to have problems when they are introduced but later turn out to have them.

Making or selling products that are known to be dangerous or harmful is unethical and it is only right that, if the supplier persists, competition or the law will soon step in. However, opinions on what should be done about products known to be dangerous to users or the environment are as varied as the evidence on the degree of danger they actually pose. This means that prejudice and misinformation cloud the ethics as much as the demands for banning or regulation. In Chapter 3 there has already been mention of two obvious examples, namely tobacco and alcohol, because so much of the debate centres round advertising and promoting them to the public.

Armaments

Mention must be made here of the very difficult subject of armaments. Most people except the most militant (*sic*) pacifists would agree that any nation has an absolute right to manufacture armaments for its defence. This then begs extraordinarily difficult questions about which weapons are defensive and which are offensive, questions that in turn depend on who asks them. Clearly, experts on military strategy will have very different views to those held by peace-loving people who are emotionally uneasy about the cost of armaments in relation, say, to healthcare. This is not the place to discuss whether appeasement pays in the face of threats from dangerous dictators, but there is a serious competitive issue in relation to exporting arms to such regimes, especially in poor countries. Regardless of that, or questions about the uses to which the arms are to be put, there is always the fear that competitors from other countries will step in anyway, with the resultant threat to jobs at home. It is not surprising that business prefers governments to regulate what they may or may not do in such cases, providing of course those same governments are honest and even-handed in the way they handle them, which is far from always the case.

Infant formula

An entirely different product, which is generally acceptable in all countries but not necessarily in all circumstances, is infant formula baby-milk substitute. In this connection, Nestlé was accused of promoting its infant formula in some developing countries as superior to breast milk, when the water with which it had to be mixed was of such poor quality that the product became positively harmful. To the campaigners who demonstrated against Nestlé, in the United States in 1977 and subsequently in other countries, the issue looked simple enough, but in fact it is much more complex. According to the company, the controversy centred round two key questions: first, whether the product was needed for more than a small minority of infants and, secondly, whether the methods used by the industry, and Nestlé in particular, to promote breast-milk substitutes were appropriate. The company agreed that it was of course arguable whether the advertising of such products to mothers in developing countries, where the supply of clean water was known to be inadequate, was indeed appropriate and that to some extent these problems could have been foreseen. Nevertheless, the criticisms of the campaigners extended far beyond this point, some of them even challenging the legitimacy of the product itself as an alternative to breast feeding.

The controversy led to intervention by the World Health Organization (WHO), which produced in 1981 an international code on the marketing of breast-milk substitutes. In the preamble to this code the WHO said: '... there is a legitimate market for infant formula and... these products should accordingly be made accessible to those who need them through commercial and non-commercial distribution systems.' This statement recognized clearly that there is no problem for mothers in any part of the world who require these products and are able to use them properly. Nestlé's own company charter (1996) on selling infant formula in developing countries (which are defined therein) specifically encourages and supports exclusive breast-feeding as the best choice for babies in the first months of life and prohibits *inter alia* advertising to the public and the distribution of free samples to mothers.

Nestlé is the first to admit that its reputation was damaged among certain groups of opinion formers (although there was no measurable commercial impact), but the exaggerated criticisms continued for years and were repeated over and over again as a general example of the misbehaviour and power of multinational companies, which was not only intellectually dishonest, because it was arguing from the particular to the general, but also became weakened by repetition.

Polyurethane foam

The extent to which the products mentioned so far, from armaments to infant formula, are unethical is clearly in the eyes of the beholder and dependent in some cases on how they are sold and how and where they are promoted. There are, however, some products that are undeniably useful, but can have problems in use that are exaggerated by ill-informed critics. One of these is polyurethane foam, which is used in large quantities in upholstery, mattresses, car seating, packaging, and many other varied applications.

In the 1970s it became clear that its otherwise excellent physical properties and versatility of use were marred by its flammability once the cover caught alight and the fact that, as it burnt, it gave off deadly toxic fumes. The product did indeed have an inherent problem, as does petrol, but people were much more ignorant about this danger than about flammable liquids and did not exercise the same level of common sense when smoking or when moving armchairs too close to open fires.

The chemical manufacturers and the foam industry worldwide invested millions of dollars in research to try to produce flame-retardant or even non-flammable foams, while there were mounting pressures on governments to legislate or even ban the use of the product. One activist in the UK, a Member of Parliament and an engineer by training, had read that foam could self-combust in the first twenty-four hours after being made in the factory, due to exothermal activity in the chemical process. He then went on television to say the product should be banned because a cushion could catch fire as you sat on it. This was clearly nonsense, but it added to the criticism of the industry every time people died in a house fire where upholstery had been the prime contributor to the tragedy.

The outcome was to introduce regulations governing the degree of flame retardance in the foam itself and the types of cover to be used. Though these measures reduce the initial risk of products catching fire, the products can still burn and, when they do, they still give off dangerous fumes, so warning labels also had to be attached to the product.

The ethical lesson of this example is that society has judged the balance of interest of the consumer, not by banning the product, but by legislating for a degree of improvement in safety and much-improved warnings to the public. One day, competition may result in an alternative product that is really non-flammable (as one manufacturer thought it had done in the mid-1970s), but experience shows that if such a breakthrough were to be achieved, the product would have other disadvantages, one of which would almost certainly be far higher costs. This is a key point that some consumer campaigners fail, or do not want, to understand: the perfect product in all respects is rare indeed.

Financial services

The examples of unsuitable or allegedly unsuitable products mentioned so far have come from manufacturing industry, but in recent years the services sector has featured more and more.

An obvious example is the overselling of endowment mortgages in the property boom of the 1980s, which was driven by the greed of both consumers and providers who thought house prices would continue upwards. Selling mortgages is highly competitive, but how they were sold at that time raised key ethical considerations that were tragically revealed when the bubble burst and millions of people were left with negative equity, repossessions and serious hardship, bringing financial hardship that in a few cases even resulted in suicide.

Should 100 per cent mortgage advances ever have been allowed? With benefit of hindsight, the more responsible building societies stopped selling them fairly early on, but it was questionable whether they should have ever been offered in the first place. True, the institutions lost enormous sums themselves for overselling mortgages, but this did not in any way mitigate their abuse of their customers.

Likewise, the attraction of large first-year commissions to salesmen of private pensions in the late 1980s led to scandalous mis-selling of products that were inappropriate to the needs of clients, many of whom lost out by switching from employee-based schemes that provided better benefits.

One of the slickest salesmen of this kind was Roger Levitt, whose company's sales grew so fast that three major British insurers and one Italian company, delighted with its apparent success, invested in it. His last published 'accounts' showed a profit on sales that no manufacturer would ever dream of. (No provision had been made in his accounts for the need to repay commission to the insurance companies when the clients to whom pensions had been oversold were no longer able to contribute to them.) The company collapsed, Levitt went on trial for fraud and received a sentence that was regarded by many as derisory (resulting from a plea bargain) and that bore no relation to the magnitude of the losses incurred by his company's clients.

More recently there have been apologies from many of the more reputable companies that mis-sold pensions, but critics have contrasted the fine words with delays in the payment of compensation.

Built-in obsolescence

Another example of products with known defects, but where judgment of the ethics is highly subjective and a question of degree, is those which suffer from built-in obsolescence.

Some products, such as computers and software, which are subject to continuous and rapid technical improvement, almost inevitably become obsolete soon after they are sold, and it would be very difficult to prove that this is a result of a deliberate policy on the part of the suppliers. However, there is a strong temptation in marketing to try to convince users that they have to renew their PCs and software more often than is strictly necessary and at the same time to make them acquire more and more 'features' which they may not really need. In this instance, where the software world market is dominated by one company, Microsoft, it is very easy to make such charges, which are then countered with the argument that the whole industry is moving so fast that constant change is the only way to maintain competitive edge.

Perhaps the most unethical products amongst those with built-in obsolescence are those that are deliberately not built to last (though of course the argument in their favour will always be based on their relatively low price), and those that are difficult to repair and for which spare parts are said to be unavailable. Many such products can be considered unethical, both from the point of view of consumers and of the environment, being an unpleasant aspect of today's throw-away society. If enough people feel strongly enough, a market may be created and competition will be able to provide superior longer-lasting products.

The problem of 'state of the art' products

Many products carry risks unknown at the time that they are brought on to the market, and they thus raise many important and highly controversial ethical questions. Any responsible company, especially where human health and safety is involved, will subject products to rigorous testing for both ethical and hard-nosed business reasons. If they do not, the results could be catastrophic, both for the company and for the people using its products, as Distillers discovered in the early 1960s when the awful effects on children born of mothers who had taken Thalidomide in pregnancy became known. But this poses the question of how much testing there should be and raises yet another well-worn issue, namely whether testing should be allowed at all on animals and, if so, under what conditions.

Sometimes highly ethical companies show self-restraint in the way in which products are promoted in the light of subsequent knowledge. Johnson & Johnson's baby oil, for instance, used to be very successful as a tanning product and, before there was great public awareness of the dangers of skin cancer from excessive exposure to the sun, their marketing people wanted to promote it as providing a 'healthy tan'. Top management took the (ethical) view that it could not prove it was 'healthy' even though at that stage there was no clearly understood evidence that it was not. Thus they decided not to allow it to be promoted on that basis, and sales fell accordingly.

In many instances, the action forced on producers by public opinion can be greatly exaggerated. The reaction to British beef, particularly in Germany, or indeed to any beef at all, because of the possibility of humans contracting Creutzfeldt-Jakob Disease from BSE-infected cattle, came to a head in 1996. The whole affair was fraught with problems relating to the difficulty of establishing adequate data on which sensible decisions could be made and suspicions of overreaction and trade protectionism. Of course health considerations were overriding, but many people took the view that products such as beef on the bone should not be banned but carry appropriate warnings, thus leaving it to individuals to decide whether to buy them or not.

The Precautionary Principle

The foregoing is a classic example of the 'Precautionary Principle', which in the last twenty years of this century has become a deeply and sincerely-held belief of environmentalists in particular. It is based on the premise that where there is doubt or lack of knowledge about the possible environmental, health or safety effects of products or processes, existing activities should be banned or reduced and new ones should not be introduced until it can be shown that there is no risk. Because the debate on the technical aspects can be highly contentious, this raises difficult ethical questions.

Taken at its extreme, the Precautionary Principle would have stifled competitive innovation and prevented a very high proportion of technical developments from taking place at all. If it had been strictly applied in the last thousand years, we might all still be living on the land, supported by a few artisans. This romantic idea is very appealing, until it is realized there would be very high infant mortality and no anaesthetics, that few of us would travel much farther than the next village and few would live beyond the age of forty. Life would, indeed, be nasty, brutish and short.

One of the greatest practical and ethical difficulties in this context is how much is known at the time of introduction about the side effects of a new product or process. Any responsible producer accepts as an ethical and commercial duty the need to establish that it poses minimal risk to the environment or to health and safety. The problem is that, even if a new product seems to be acceptable at the time, later evidence might show this not to be the case. In other words, 'the state of the art' knowledge might not be adequate and therefore might not be acceptable.

One of the clearest examples of this problem was the use of CFCs in cooling processes. When they were introduced, CFCs were shown to give their makers competitive edge because they were extremely useful, relatively inexpensive to make and non-toxic into the bargain. It was only many years later that scientists concluded that they were damaging the earth's ozone layer. Once that was proved beyond reasonable doubt, leading manufacturers agreed with governments that they should be phased out. This has proved more easily agreed than done, and CFCs are still being traded in certain countries.

From the business point of view, the Precautionary Principle can therefore only be accepted up to a certain point. After that, there is need for pragmatism. This view was reflected in the *Business Charter for Sustainable Development*, the joint commitment to continuous improvement drawn up and published by the International Chamber of Commerce (ICC) in 1991, a year before the Rio Earth Summit. In that code, the phrase 'Precautionary Approach' was used and was defined in the following words: 'To modify the manufacture, marketing or use of products or services or the conduct of activities, consistent with scientific and technical understanding, to prevent serious or irreversible environmental degradation.' The emphasis here is on avoiding known risks, not hypothetical ones unsupported by scientific evidence.

The debate about global warming is the best-known case in point. Environmentalists have tended to argue that there was a scientifically proven chain reaction between fossil-fuel emissions, especially those of carbon dioxide, leading to global warming, which would in turn lead to disastrous climatic change. The only solution, as they saw it, was for massive reductions in such emissions to be agreed at Rio. Most of them were disappointed in the Rio Convention on Climate Change, and yet many sections of industry, especially the producers of coal, gas and oil, were emphatic that there were too many scientific uncertainties and that objective cost–benefit analysis showed that the measurable economic costs would heavily outweigh the evidently speculative benefits of slowing down global warming.

The arguments between governments about which countries should commit themselves to what reductions by when was the dominant feature in the years leading up to the Kyoto conference in 1998 and beyond, with the US government apparently dragging its feet, partly because of heavy lobbying by the Global Climate Coalition (GCC). BP had already deemed it appropriate to distance itself from this lobby group and withdrew from it in 1997; Shell did so the following year. While still thinking that scientific understanding of climate change was incomplete, Shell, according to its Chairman, Mark Moody-Stuart, appeared to have a 'fundamental difference of opinion' with the GCC over the ratification of the Kyoto Protocol on climate change. This was the main reason for that firm's resignation from a body that a British journalist, Graham Searjeant of The Times, described as 'antediluvian', though following their experiences over Brent Spa (see Chapter 7) Shell were probably more sensitive than they had been previously to public perceptions over such questions.

It is not only industry that is cautious about the Precautionary Principle. Even the most highly principled consumers find it difficult to pay premium prices for products that they are told will be of some benefit to the environment and to future generations but not immediately to them. When catalytic converters were first introduced on cars, many environmentally aware people were prepared to pay a premium for a car that had one fitted, but the majority waited until they were made mandatory. In contrast, the public was more rapidly converted to using marginally more environmentally friendly unleaded petrol instead of the leaded varieties when governments decided to tax the former at a lower rate than the latter.

Conclusion and advice on product problems

Individuals working in companies promoting unsuitable products need to take great care to differentiate between those that are absolutely unacceptable to them personally, in which case they should not be working there at all, and those that are being promoted to inappropriate markets, in which case they should stand up for what they believe to be right. In cases where unsuitability is a highly subjective matter, they need to consider where they themselves stand on it. Finally, in cases where 'unsuitability' is judged by opponents of business or through mere ignorance, they should stand up for their products and try to put the record straight.

Companies and individuals have a clear and obvious responsibility to see that new products are adequately tested so as to ensure they are safe and fit for the purpose for which they are to be sold. This is both an ethical necessity and common prudence, because failure to do so can be very costly, and damaging to the reputation of the company.

As far as built-in obsolescence is concerned, companies should consider whether there are not real marketing opportunities to introduce more products that last longer, can be easily repaired and for which spare parts are readily available. A growing number of consumers would be prepared to pay the higher prices (within reason) that such products would rightly command.

PRICING POLICIES

Few ethical issues relating to competition are more subject to paradox than that of pricing. In the Middle Ages there were endless religious and philosophical debates about the 'just price'. The most likely ways in which unjust prices can be charged is when there is extreme shortage (as in wartime), when black markets flourish and supply is controlled by traders or manufacturers with monopolies. This is one of the only instances where rationing and price control have to be used, it being understood that the best solution in such situations is the re-establishment of effective competition as soon as practicable.

Pricing to what the market will bear

Pricing to what the market will bear, not directly related to production cost, appears unethical to many people who are not familiar with the realities of business. Manufacturing industry very often has to charge high prices for new products which have been subject to significant development and pre-production costs, and need initially high returns so that further research can be financed. Later on, the price may well come down because these initial costs have been recouped and competition has appeared on the market.

Similarly, department store buyers will very often look at a product and say to themselves: 'I can sell that for £19. 99' and only then make the purchasing decision. In other words, there is no 'cost-plus' element in the approach. It may be that the margin will be high because the product is new to the market, but as competition develops the mark-up – and thus the margin – usually comes down.

Apart from anything else, 'cost' has much more to it than the delivered price to the retail outlet. If an item, such as a certain kind of furniture, is slow-moving, the mark-up needs to be greater to cover the space occupied and the capital tied up in keeping it in stock. If on the other hand the item is perishable, the mark-up has to cover likely waste. There are many other less obvious costs, which the following example will show.

A young European management trainee in a department store in Trinidad was horrified to see the mark-up on some women's hats that had recently arrived from Europe. He raised the matter with his manager, who smiled and said: 'Do you realize how much pilferage there is at the docks, before the merchandise reaches us at all? Quite apart from what women will pay for the hats that they want to be seen wearing in church next Sunday, we have to allow for that.' The manager went on: 'Shoes are an even worse problem: of course we bring in the whole range of sizes of men's shoes from reputable European manufacturers, but the dockers always pinch the size sevens and eights.'

Double pricing

Setting prices artificially high in order to discount is ethically much more questionable. In the Middle East and many other parts of the world this is standard practice and the locals and many visitors enjoy the process of haggling. Others do not, often because of temperament or laziness; as a result, they are ripped off by the trader. In the UK this practice, sometimes known as 'double pricing', was particularly common with products such as beds, soft furnishings and some electrical goods, an especially large proportion of which were sold in sales. Here, of course, was the classic need for the consumer to use common sense and buy on the basis of the net price, rather than be bemused by the discounts – which have in the past been known to exceed 80 per cent. In other words, this is another case where the principle of *caveat emptor* should apply.

The UK bedding industry in the 1970s was divided into three main camps: the out-and-out 'double pricers' (which tended to be at the lower end of the market), a number of neutrals in the middle, and a few anti-'double pricers' that tended to be in the upper ranges of the market and that thought such high discounts damaged their brand name. The last category made representations to the Office of Fair Trading, and as a result regulations were introduced that double price tickets were only allowable in shops if the product had been displayed for a month previously at the full price.

Subsequently the Price Commission also published a report on the subject. It showed that some shops had beds on special offer for most of the year, because double pricing was considered an essential marketing tool, and that the main purpose of setting recommended prices was to discount them. A mere eight per cent of beds were sold at these prices, and discounts of 30 per cent or more were the norm. The Price Commission concluded that the practice of double pricing at the point of sale and in media advertising should be prohibited 'except for prescribed sales periods of limited duration' and that recommended retail prices for beds should also be prohibited.

The Consumer Protection Act 1987 outlawed misleading prices and laid down that price comparisons of the sort mentioned above could only be made if the higher price had actually been charged. A government Code of Practice, which included appropriate guidelines on the subject, was published the following year and updated on matters of detail in 1997. The essence was that the higher price had to have been available for 28 consecutive days in the last six months. Here, therefore, was an example of regulation stepping in where voluntary ethical price practices had proved ineffective.

Loss leaders

Paradoxically, low pricing can sometimes be as unethical as the practices already mentioned. Distinction has to be made between 'loss leaders', which are designed to bring the customer into the shop to buy fully-priced merchandise, and 'predatory pricing', which is sustained price-cutting from a powerful company, usually aimed at achieving substantial market share at the expense of its weaker competitors.

There is nothing unethical about loss leaders. In fact the consumer can, and sometimes does, 'cherry pick' by taking advantage of the special offer and then leaving the shop. Some accountancy firms have been accused of 'low balling', that is, quoting an artificially low price for an audit, in the hope of picking up other business from the client. In this case, the situation is rather different, because once they have established themselves with a company in this way, it is often less practicable to invite a different firm to provide the other services.

Predatory pricing

On the other hand, there have been some well documented cases of 'predatory pricing', where a company goes all out to gain market share from smaller competitors through cut-price goods or services operating at a loss or only covering marginal cost. This is another case of where the consumer can reap short-term benefit but where in the final analysis the weaker competitors might be forced out of the market and competition reduced.

Elaine Sternberg, in her book *Just Business*, vigorously defended predatory pricing in the following terms: ' "Predatory" pricing which forces competitors out of business is also perfectly acceptable. Ordinary decency no more requires a business to be gentle with its competitors than it requires it to be charitable with its customers,' and she then went on to say that 'the business's obligations are to its owners, not to its competitors'. However, she qualified her hard line by saying that account has to be taken of the knock-on effects of such policies, including the fact that higher margins resulting from reduced competition may draw in new competitors and that 'public disapproval of competitive practices might lead to stakeholder alienation or competitor litigation or official regulation'.

Many readers will find it very hard to agree with Sternberg's line of argument, which only goes to show how difficult it is to be dogmatic about such matters and how unwise it is to try to generalize on questions that have to be judged case by case by the people involved at the time.

There are instances where low-pricing policies are alleged by critics (and competitors) to be 'predatory' but are defended by those involved on the grounds of the additional volume of turnover achieved, which genuinely reduces the cost of the product. An interesting example comes from the early 1990s where, in September 1993 and following a period of gradual decline in circulation of the quality daily broadsheet newspapers, News International's *The Times* decided to cut its price from 45p to 30p and then, in June 1994, to 20p. In the two following years, partly because of increases in newsprint costs, it rose again to 35p, then fell again on some days to 30p, while on some Mondays 10p only was charged. This put enormous pressure on the *Independent*, which at the beginning complained that Rupert Murdoch (head of News International) was trying to put it out of business, and on *The Daily Telegraph*, which was said to be his main target because it had the highest circulation of the three. As a result, both the other two made price cuts themselves, but never down to the same levels as *The Times*.

Much care has to be taken in interpreting the figures in the table below. For example, it is far from clear to what extent they include copies that were given away free, and there is furious dispute about the validity of the figures from the newspapers themselves and the bodies that study them; moreover, the picture seems to change each time new figures are published. However, up to December 1997 it is clear enough that *The Times* doubled its sales – a far higher increase than some of the pundits projected – while *The Daily Telegraph* made a slight gain, the *Guardian* largely retained its own particular readership, and the *Independent* declined substantially.

Was this a case of predatory pricing? Certainly the *Independent* thought so, and with some reason. Asked what he thought of these allegations of supporters of the *Independent*, a leading *Times* journalist said that News International's actions had been justified on commercial grounds, but he added drily that he was glad he didn't work for the *Independent*.

The strongest arguments in favour of this latter view are that in the period illustrated above the total market for the four newspapers together increased by 16 per cent, and no more than a quarter of *The Times*'s increases could be said to have been made at the expense of the *Independent*. Moreover, if it is true that only about 30 per cent of the revenue of *The Times* is supposed to come from the cover price and the rest from advertising, the increase in sales and the concomitant increase in advertising copy may have compensated for the drop in cover prices. The question also arises as to whether *The Times* in fact *ever* makes money and whether its actions are being supported by cross-subsidization from other parts of Rupert Murdoch's empire.

Interestingly, *The Times* reported early in 1998 that the *Guardian* was 'moving in for the kill' on the *Independent* by mailing its readers with special offers, when the latter thought that the *Guardian* and it were together supposed to be 'fighting the might of Rupert Murdoch'. There is also a theory that *The Daily Telegraph* is in fact the main target of *The Times* in the long term, and the latter seemed to go out of its way to confirm this view when it published data from the ABC to show how it was 'fast closing the gap on *The [Daily] Telegraph*'.

Average net sales (000s) of broadsheet newspapers, 1992–97

Period	The Daily Telegraph	The Independent	The Guardian	The Times	Total
July–December 1992	1,036	368	413	379	2,196
January–June 1993	1,025	347	416	366	2,154
July–December 1993	1,017	324	399	412	2,152
January–June 1994	1,008	281	403	485	2,177
July–December 1994	1,075	281	399	604	2,359
January–June 1995	1,066	294	400	647	2,407
July–December 1995	1,053	293	395	669	2,410
January–June 1996	1,044	279	398	685	2,406
July–December 1996	1,084	265	397	791	2,537
January–June 1997	1,125	257	409	748	2,539
July–December 1997	1,098	260	404	792	2,554
Change (Jan–June 1993 = 100)	106	71	98	209	116

Source: ABC

Price is, of course, only part of a story that will run on for some years. Comparisons, for example, must include the relative qualty of the products themselves. Commentators will always be able to find evidence to support their own prejudices and readers must be left to draw their own conclusions.

As a footnote it is worth noting that *The Daily Telegraph* set a precedent for all this in 1930 when it halved its cover price from twopence to a penny while *The Times* remained at twopence. In two weeks *The Daily Telegraph* almost doubled its circulation from 100,000 to 190,000, some of it at the expense of *The Times*. So, what's new?

Should predatory pricing be made illegal? One journalist wrote in the *Independent* that it was a 'joyful time' when the House of Lords voted in early 1998 for the inclusion of the outlawing of this practice in the Competition Bill before

Parliament, but the government's attitude was that existing rules were adequate. Apart from anything else, the complications of gathering evidence and proving that pricing policies are predatory are always formidable.

Conclusion and advice on pricing problems

In view of all that has been said on the question of pricing, there is little advice that can usefully be given to companies or individuals responsible for pricing policies. Much of the criticism of some of the pricing practices encountered in business comes from people from outside business, whose main objective is to try to show that business is by its very nature immoral.

However, companies and individuals of integrity should take great care in such matters as 'double pricing' and avoid real 'predatory pricing', which is deliberately aimed at the elimination of competitors and therefore a reduction in the very competition that this book is intended to celebrate.

PURCHASING

There are some aspects of commercial relationships that raise important ethical questions, but that are not always covered by codes of practice. When the customer is much larger than the supplier, there is special need to balance highly competitive purchasing power with appropriate responsibility and restraint in how it is exercised. The obvious example is the relationship between the large chains of retail stores and their suppliers.

Volume and price

One of the main problems of excessive purchasing power relates to volume and price. The smaller supplier can be forced down to very low margins related to the prospect of large orders which, if they are not forthcoming, can cause the supplier severe problems. If the orders do come, then the supplier may find that too much capacity is devoted to a single customer; if the orders are intimated but not formally contracted for, then the supplier's capacity may be expanded on the basis of possible, but not certain, future business. Responsible large retailers recognize these difficulties.

For example, in the 1950s, a leading Canadian department store imported merchandise on a large scale from Europe. The sports goods buyers were seeking high-quality hand-made leather ski boots and found an excellent supplier in Austria that only employed about a dozen people. A small order was placed at the price asked, but the buyers offered to buy a much larger quantity at a much lower price. The proprietor of the supplying company was very tempted to accept the larger order, but one of the buying team took him aside and advised him to think carefully before he put most of his eggs into the one basket. He wisely opted for the smaller order and continued to supply his existing customers elsewhere. The following year the Canadian company switched its source of supply to an Italian firm that was much better able to handle the higher volume required.

One way in which large retail chains can hold their suppliers to ransom (whether they are small or not) is to get them to help finance special in-store promotions in return for shelf space, particularly at those key positions at the end of each aisle. Indeed, even giants such as Unilever and Nestlé, in spite of their own size, can suffer from the big retailers' very high share of their market and consequent buying power. In these circumstances, even if national market shares show a reasonable balance between manufacturers and retailers, a strong retailer presence at regional level can produce very anti-competitive results.

Furthermore, a decision to drop a branded line in favour of an own-branded product can affect the supplier very badly. It is notable that Kellogg's, which as a matter of policy does not manufacture retailers' own brands of breakfast cereals, advertises the fact to the public so as to differentiate its products from those of the retailers.

Some manufacturers find it ironical that competition law is almost invariably aimed at them, the suppliers, rather than at the market dominance of some retailers, the political justification being that the consumer is the ultimate beneficiary. There is no doubt that in the UK in the mid-1990s the ferocious competition between Sainsbury and Tesco, with Safeway and a revived Asda following behind, did bring notable consumer benefits but, as already mentioned in Chapter 2, their strength in the market brought further pressure on small shops as well as on suppliers.

'Just-in-time' delivery

'Just-in-time' delivery requirements – another aspect of the relationship between customers, whether they are retailers or manufacturers, and their suppliers – have brought great pressure on the latter whatever their size. These delivery arrangements benefit the customer by keeping inventories down, but can have the reverse effect on suppliers if they are to ensure good service. Charles Handy also remarks that this system increases the number of half-filled trucks on the road and is thus detrimental to traffic movement and to the environment.

Payments to suppliers

Timely payment to suppliers is another well-worn subject. Strong buying power enables customers to extract excessively long payment terms from suppliers. This can then be compounded by deliberately late payment (especially unethical when the supplier is a small company and in no position to object), a practice which has been rightly condemned by many politicians and business organizations.

The practice was described in the CBI's Watkinson Report of 1973 as 'an abuse of power and morally indefensible', and the CBI has continued to make such statements ever since. Most recently, the problem has been of concern to politicians worried about the problems of small companies. During 1997 the UK government issued consultative documents on the subject, and by Spring 1998 the Late Payment of Commercial Debts (Interest) Bill was making its way through Parliament.

Conclusion and advice on purchasing power

All the matters mentioned above, where the pressures between customers and their competitors on the one hand and suppliers and their competitors on the other, pose many ethical questions that affect purchasing and finance departments.

Few company codes specifically address the issue of how their purchasing power should be exercised, especially in relation to smaller suppliers. In most cases the concern is for the integrity of purchasing departments in resisting inducements to favour one supplier over another, as already covered in detail in the previous chapter. How much an individual company exercises its power depends on the moral culture set from the top.

It is good business to value good suppliers; it is also ethical to deal with them fairly. Ideally, they should be treated as valued partners and respected accordingly. This is spelt out in detail in Chapter 7.

PEOPLE

Treatment of employees

Though this is quite obviously a moral question, some people would ask what it has to do with competition. It is included here because many companies blame the pressures of competition for the measures they take to reduce the costs of employing people. There was an announcement to this effect by British Airways the very day these lines were written. Taken separately, most companies are able to justify such measures and would certainly reject the view that they are acting improperly.

Companies have to be able to make people redundant as situations change and new technologies are introduced. At one time, many companies went on employing people who were not needed for one reason or another. They were moved into non-jobs until they could retire with due dignity. Competition has ensured that this is no longer acceptable, and indeed it must be unethical to put the company – and therefore the jobs of the rest of the employees – at risk by retaining unnecessary extra employment costs. Provided those people who are no longer needed are given counselling and understanding, together with sever-ance terms that are preferably better than those laid down by law, redundancy has to be accepted as a fact of life and in theory companies have no further moral responsibility.

But there are companies that still do their utmost to avoid such eventualities. One such is the John Lewis Partnership. The Chairman, Stuart Hampson, made a remarkable speech at the Institute of Directors Annual Convention in 1997 in which he said: 'If you think of employees as a resource to be utilized as re-quired, to be discarded when times get hard, to be downsized or re-engineered, then don't be surprised if they behave like it.'

Even if redundancies are deemed absolutely necessary, ethical questions arise on how the rest of the workforce is treated. One of the main worries of the critics of business morality is the transference of so many jobs to part-time or self-employment, with pension and protection rights very inferior to those en-joyed by full-time employees.

Over the years too many UK companies have cut training budgets whenever they were faced with competitive and cost pressures. In the past, there was re-sentment about government's training levies, which should not have been nec-essary with adequate commitment to training in the first place. This is in contrast to countries like Germany, where apprenticeship schemes and other training continue to be given high priority because of a recognition that short-term savings in this area are unjustified on both ethical and longer-term competitive grounds.

In addition, the truly horrible word 'downsizing' means that those who re-main in their jobs generally have to work harder than ever, with the additional pressure of increased worry that they may be the next to go. Charles Handy, in *The Empty Raincoat*, deplored the fact that in advanced countries competition means employing fewer people, paid more and producing much more. He quoted the neglected spouse of a very well-paid but overworked banker who said: 'It's a crazy system. It doesn't make sense. Why don't they employ twice as many people at half the salary and work them half as hard? That way they could all lead a normal life.' Handy's comment on this is 'But they don't, and they won't and they can't, not if they want to remain competitive.' He states that it makes good corporate sense to minimize staffing levels as described, but his worry is the damage it does to the quality of life of the people involved.

The growth of evidence of stress in workforces – at all levels and not just at the top – has exercised many writers. It was addressed by the Institute of Business Ethics in its 1995 publication *Employees' Health and Organisational Practice*, which begs the question of whether the trend is going too far, to the extent that it is beginning to be counter-productive for companies. A different concern is that the savage reduction of corporate head offices (most of which were indeed overmanned) means that there are now too few people left with the time to *think*. This in turn can result in short-termism and inadequate strategic policy-making.

The worry of many commentators is that reductions in numbers employed by businesses has widened the gap between the haves and the have-nots in society. This is Will Hutton's thesis in *The State We're In,* when he calls the UK a '30-30-40 society' – 30 per cent 'disadvantaged' in not having work; 30 per cent 'marginalized and insecure', being in casual or part-time work or recently self-employed; and 40 per cent 'privileged' by being in longer-term self-employment or permanent jobs. As ever, it is not all bad news, because even Hutton admits that for many people, especially men and women with children to look after, part-time or self-employment is the ideal solution.

The economic benefits and social disadvantages of the relatively flexible labour markets of the UK and the US, in contrast with the social market economies of countries such as Sweden, Germany and France, are highly relevant to the debate about international competitiveness. It will be very difficult to reach a clear consensus as to which approach is economically and ethically superior, but the optimistic view is that the two approaches will continue to draw closer to each other, thus retaining the best aspects of each.

Perhaps the worst moral action of all is the exploitation for competitive reasons of the underprivileged in developing countries, which has already been covered briefly in the section on protectionism in Chapter 2.

'Excessive' pay for business leaders

This question generated a great deal of heat in the UK, especially in 1995–96. The standard argument in favour of very high rates of pay is that companies need to attract the best people for competitive reasons, and ethically there is no problem here at all. Much of the fury of the media on this subject was generated by old-fashioned envy, which is an aspect of anti-business culture – there is much less adverse comment about the earnings of pop stars or top sports performers. Interestingly, pay differentials generate less concern in the United States, with its tradition of greater social and economic mobility.

However, two words in the title of this subsection underline the real ethical problem. The word 'excessive' can be purely subjective, but frequently refers, rightly, to the circumstances in which a pay increase is awarded. Subjectivity, in turn, is supposed to be avoided because remuneration committees (where they exist) are made up of non-executive directors. The problem here is that the latter have in most cases been invited to serve by the people they are rewarding, while some of them have those same people on their boards as non-executives, so that there is always the suspicion of incestuous reciprocal favours.

The word 'leaders' should not be subjective at all. The ethics of leadership are based on the age-old principle that privileges must be matched by responsibility to the led. For top business people to allow their remuneration to be substantially increased, either when the company is not performing to objectively improved standards, or when profitability has increased on the back of massive redundancies of staff and strict limits on the pay of the remaining employees, is at best insensitive and at worst a total abrogation of what leadership is about. Unfortunately there is a minority of people in top positions in business who are out for all they can get for themselves and care little about those who work under them.

In a statement produced in 1995 to coincide with the work of the Greenbury Committee, which was set up in the UK to make recommendations on this question, the then Chairman of the Institute of Business Ethics, Neville Cooper, wrote:

> ... pay and benefits should be economically justifiable and, in a market economy, subject to market forces. In addition, however, regard must be paid to people's perceptions, which can affect social issues. Leadership must include responsibility for the consequences of one's actions. In some cases this may involve no more than careful explanation. In general, the most successful and well-run companies encounter the least criticism over executive pay and these often give the clearest statement of the facts.

Indeed, the ethical necessity is for far greater disclosure, far more transparency in these matters, to ensure that increases are justified by the fulfilment of targets that are demanding and have been set in advance. In the early stages when the issue of executive pay came to the fore, most of the protests came from private shareholders who could make a lot of noise at Annual General Meetings, but who had inadequate voting clout to make any difference. As the institutional shareholders have taken a hand, the situation has begun to change.

However, these developments do not take care of the problems of leadership, including the moral dilemma facing directors whose results are achieved wholly or largely on the back of redundancies and restraints on the levels of pay of their employees. Here, sound company values and the consciences of individuals still have a key part to play.

Finance versus factory – the problem of differentials

Ethical questions about pay also apply to certain employees in the financial sector, mainly in the City of London. Six-figure remuneration enjoyed by often very young people working in stressful and insecure jobs is usually justified on competitive grounds. At times these rates of pay have been further inflated by 'golden hellos' to lure staff from competitors. As in the case of top people, critics are often accused of feelings of envy, especially if they are unemployed or marginalized.

But to people in manufacturing industry, earning only a fraction of the remuneration of their contemporaries in the City, the justification of competition is hard to accept. For example, Britain has been notorious since the Second World War for the low social status and pay available to engineers, in stark contrast to other countries, especially Germany, where the title *Herr Ingenieur* really counts. It is hard to prove, but there is a view that competition between industry and services has resulted in too many good people being lured to the latter at the expense of the former.

Poaching trained staff

Some companies are notorious for their practice of recruiting people of all levels who have been trained by competitors, thus avoiding themselves the expense of training those new employees. This practice tends to be the subject of anecdotal evidence and therefore very hard to pin down as a deliberate policy rather than normal competitive recruitment of suitably qualified people.

The practice of poaching is nevertheless worth mentioning here because, if it becomes too widespread, companies can be faced with a further incentive to cut back on training, apart from the usual reason of saving money in times of recession. Training has been very inadequate in UK business in the last two decades of the twentieth century, so any disincentive of this kind is greatly to the disadvantage of both individual employees and business itself.

Conclusion and advice on people problems

Ethics and normal good management of people belong firmly together. Good leadership, transparency and a sensitivity to the perceptions of employees are essential. Above all, there is a very strong ethical and practical case for treating people as the most precious asset that a company can have. This adds to a company's long-term competitiveness, as is argued in Chapter 7.

INTELLIGENCE GATHERING AND INDUSTRIAL ESPIONAGE

This is an aspect of competition where the grey areas between legitimate intelligence-gathering on competitors and acts involving theft and trespass are often subject to individual judgment and the exercise of personal conscience. While it may be both immoral and illegal to steal prototypes not yet on the market, or formulae and documents related to takeover bids, there can be circumstances where information comes from, say, a disaffected employee and the morality of acting on it can only be judged by case.

Intelligence gathering

There may be nothing wrong with acting on information received through the incompetence of another party. This can occur between whole industries in different countries. For example, in 1979 the Japanese could have had a valuable windfall of market intelligence on the British motor components industry from a quango appointed by the British Government, and it would have cost them the princely sum of £3.

The quango in question was the Price Commission, which was charged with conducting detailed investigations into the price structures of products considered to be sensitive in the marketplace. Their last investigation before they were disbanded was to investigate in depth the cost structures right through the supply chain, from raw materials to the finished product bought by consumers, of 17 selected car parts ranging from tyres to oil filters. Members of the Commission were not a little surprised to be warned by industry representatives that this information would be of inestimable value to Japanese competitors. While they had a statutory duty to conduct the investigation in full, they were persuaded to leave blank many of the key supporting tables in the published report (price £3), thus reducing the exercise to well deserved absurdity.

The paradox of this example is that, while the government of the day felt that they were on the side of the angels in trying to curb inflation with the aid of the Price Commission, they nearly provided detailed market intelligence to overseas competitors, which the latter would have had every ethical justification in using.

There are also cases where industrial intelligence received because of the mistakes of others can present the people involved with moral dilemmas. For instance, by mistake a solicitor sent documents to a company lawyer that were intended for the other side in a legal suit. Rather than returning them immediately, the recipient read them and then reported on them to his chairman. The latter saw this as a breach of professional ethics and shortly afterwards the lawyer left the company.

Information can be misdirected deliberately, as in the case of the MD of a company with branches in rented premises all over a country in continental Europe being faced with stiff competition and having to do all he could to contain costs. He heard that the landlord of two of the branches was thinking of asking for a rent increase in the hope that the company would prefer to avoid the cost of finding new premises, removal expenses and disruption to trade. The MD dictated a letter to one of the branch managers instructing him to start looking at once for alternative premises at a rent no higher that that being paid at present. He told his secretary to put the letter in an envelope addressed to the landlord instead of the branch manager. When the landlord telephoned to say what had happened, the MD expressed astonishment, followed by anger at the 'incompetence' of his office, but no more was heard of the rent review.

The reader must be left to judge the nuances of morality in these two instances, but they do show that the use of sensitive information received by accident must be a matter of individual conscience – and that sometimes such information can be misleading.

There are plenty of examples of absolutely legitimate and routine intelligence gathering. One is the normal practice of retailers using anonymous shoppers to check prices and service levels among their competitors, or companies in manufacturing and service industries analysing in detail the policies, products and marketing practices of other companies in the same field. Normally these do not give rise to moral problems.

Industrial espionage

Outright industrial espionage is quite a different matter. Because of its very nature, it is extremely hard to quote concrete examples, but concerns about the bugging of offices of competitors are so common that it has become not uncommon since the 1970s for larger companies to 'sweep' their offices for bugs before sensitive matters are discussed at meetings. This is particularly serious if the information so acquired can affect the share price or when disputed takeovers are being discussed in the offices of the potential quarry, the predator or the financial advisers of both parties.

Industrial espionage is often undertaken on behalf of companies by private detectives using all sorts of sophisticated equipment. There have even been cases where searching through dustbins has provided useful information, a practice which some would regard as ethically acceptable.

In a strange twist of English law, the Theft Act 1968 did not apply to documentary trade secrets, however valuable. This absurd anomaly meant that the theft of the paper that the secrets were written on was the only crime, not the ideas or other information that the papers contained, in contrast to the situation applying to infringements of copyright. Civil remedies were considered insufficient as many of the people stealing secrets would have insufficient assets to satisfy a court ruling. In view of this weakness in English law, the UK Law Commission published in 1997 a consultation paper, *Misuse of Trade Secrets* (LCCP 150), as a step towards strengthening it and legislation was planned. In several other countries, including France, Germany and most states in the US, criminal sanctions can already be applied against the misuse of confidential business information.

Where the law is defective, company codes of ethics have a particular role to play. As is so often the case, some of the best examples come from the US. For example, Du Pont makes a very clear distinction between acceptable and unacceptable intelligence gathering:

> The business world is highly competitive and success in it demands an understanding of competitors' strategies. While collecting data on our competitors, we should utilize all legitimate resources, but avoid those actions which are illegal, unethical or which could cause embarrassment to Du Pont.

Some companies deliberately recruit people from competitor companies solely to get information from them. The best-known recent example occurred in Germany in 1994 and was widely reported by the media. José Ignacio López, the purchasing chief of Opel, the German subsidiary of General Motors (GM), was recruited by Volkswagen together with some of his colleagues. The matter came before the German courts, where the prosecution alleged that they brought with them computer printouts containing details of the components that Opel was buying, including the prices paid. 'It was', wrote Christian Tyler in *The Financial Times*, 'as if Opel had been stripped naked in the market place.' This case had many ramifications, but one of them was that Volkswagen agreed out of court to pay GM $100 million in damages and to buy $1 billion's worth of parts from them in the next seven years.

An example of a company that specifically prohibits any practice of this kind, as well as espionage in general, is IBM. The Conduct Guidelines of IBM UK state:

> No company should employ improper means to acquire a competitor's trade secrets or other confidential information. Such flagrant practices as industrial espionage, burglary, wire tapping and stealing are obviously wrong. But so is hiring a competitor's employees solely to get confidential information. Improper solicitation of confidential data from a competitor's employees or from IBM customers is wrong. IBM will not tolerate any form of questionable intelligence-gathering.

Conclusion and advice on intelligence gathering

The whole question of espionage and intelligence gathering is far from easy. It ranges from the outright black illegal and immoral) through the usual grey areas (the difficult part) to the white (the acceptable and legitimate). Guidance is needed, above all, on where to draw the line on what is, and what is not, acceptable.

This is an aspect of competition where well thought-out and adequately promulgated company codes are the best way of providing guidance to employees. Companies that turn their backs on facing this question run the risk of putting their own employees in impossible situations. The IBM code quoted above is an excellent example, or for wider advice the guidance of a body such as the Institute of Business Ethics may be sought.

Individuals' first recourse should therefore be to the company's code or other guidelines. If there is no such code, then there is much to be said for pressing for guidelines to be produced before a possible need for them should arise. If there is no support provided by the company, people of principle once again have to act in accordance with their own consciences, even to the extent of putting their jobs at risk.

Chapter 6

Facing the dilemmas

'If only it were true that the problems I face daily in business were only dilemmas,' said the chief executive. 'In reality, the difficult decisions I have to make are much more complicated than a choice between two courses of action.' So it is in the case of the ethical problems faced by individuals of principle as they struggle for their companies and their own careers in the face of the white heat of competition in the marketplace.

In theory, a course of action can be ruled out because it is against the law and a decision to do so can be made out of mere prudence and not on moral grounds at all. This begs the question of what principled people should do when superiors or colleagues take decisions to break the law, either out of ignorance or deliberately in the hope that they will not be found out. It is more difficult when an action is taken that seems to be sailing very close to the wind as far as the law is concerned. It becomes even more difficult when such a move is legal but is still seen to be immoral. Any two colleagues in a company can view a given situation in quite different ways. They can each see it as a matter of personal judgment, subject to their own individual moral standards, and may also have very different ideas on its justification in practical business terms.

Thus the imperatives of competition can lead to creative morality. The easy way out is to stay quiet, above all when taking a stand may jeopardize a career or job. Personal prudence can lead only too easily to moral turpitude.

The purpose of this chapter is to examine what help is open to companies and individuals to enable them to conform to moral principles and support the dictates of their consciences. It looks at the law and discusses the case both in its favour and for leaving as much as is practical and effective to self-regulation within a framework of law. Different aspects of self-regulation are examined with particular reference to those elements of company codes of ethics which are most relevant to competition.

THE ROLE OF THE LAW

In the context of this book, there are two diametrically opposed schools of thought on the role of the law in business practice. On the one hand there are those in the business world who believe in the maximum possible self-regulation, whose views are reflected in the pages that follow. On the other hand there are those who distrust market principles and believe, quite simply, that business never does anything, or refrains from any action, that may jeopardize profit unless forced to do so by regulations or the threat of sanctions. This latter school of thought includes socialist writers and economists, some Keynesians, consumer campaigners such as the veteran Ralph Nader and, in the present day, some of the more extreme environmentalists. A contemporary journalist, Will Hutton, says that deregulation turns only too easily into licence.

Traditionally, as has been discussed in Chapter 2, the most significant legislation directly governing competition is that directed at preventing market dominance or collusion in the marketplace. The reason it has become so significant is that the temptations enunciated by Adam Smith are believed to be so strong that competition is simply prevented from working as it should. According to T L Beauchamp in *Ethical Theory and Business*, Adam Smith recognized the need for a 'minimal state... to provide and enforce the rules of the competitive game', and even Milton Friedman approved of it.

In our complex society, a mixture of national and international laws, conventions and institutions must be brought to bear on the way that companies compete with one another. Business people themselves, as indicated in several places in this book already, often prefer and even seek regulation in order to prohibit unfair practices by competitors and establish a more level playing field.

Very frequently companies can gain competitive advantage by anticipating future regulations which they believe to be inevitable. This gives them a head start in achieving compliance in a controlled manner, in contrast to competitors who wait until they are hit by the requirements of the law. This has been especially true in the last three decades of the century in connection with the growing body of law governing the environment.

Sometimes the advantage can favour a whole nation. German companies were initially very concerned at the additional costs forced on them by the powerful campaigning of their own environmentalists, but subsequently they had a big advantage over their competitors in other EU countries because Environmental Directives from Brussels followed the German model and their exports of appropriate equipment benefited accordingly.

Many matters, if they are perceived to be important enough, require regulation, most especially products that are environmentally desirable but involve significant additional costs. The example of catalytic converters has already been mentioned in Chapter 5. They were fitted to some of the more expensive models ahead of legal requirements but needed the force of legislation before becoming standard on cheaper cars.

Limitations of the law

From the point of view of business people faced with hard moral decisions, the law can indeed be helpful in establishing clear rules (that is, assuming they *are* clear), but it also carries with it a number of limitations, some of which even the most ardent believers in business regulation have to admit are true.

■ The law is essentially reactive. It can never be up-to-date, especially in matters where developing technology is involved. By definition, it cannot be at the leading edge.

■ If there is too much law, managements have to spend so much time ensuring compliance that they have correspondingly less time and resources to do other things. Larger companies wisely pay highly qualified people to monitor compliance, but in smaller companies this has to be left to directors and owners and they have many other things to worry about. It is particularly necessary in the case of environmental matters, where excessive law can result in a diversion of research and process resources away from the achievement of the big technical breakthroughs which are beyond the imagination and understanding of lawmakers. (One of the most environmentally significant inventions of the twentieth century was optical fibres. No law demanded their invention, yet the advantages they have brought to the environment have far exceeded the benefits of much legislation introduced for similar purposes.)

■ The bureaucracy associated with the law can be a disincentive to smaller new entrants into the marketplace and therefore a restraint on competition. (As the next section shows, it has to be admitted that this problem can apply to self-regulation as well.)

■ The law is usually too rigid and too blunt an instrument to cover all situations in all sorts of businesses without being overprescriptive and bureaucratic. As it is, the additional safeguards required by law in financial services, for example, have added greatly to administration and therefore costs.

■ The law, and the fear of it, induces much too much caution and secrecy in companies. Very often, and most especially in the US, where lawyers play a significant role in determining policies, companies are often inhibited in communicating with the public as they should do on matters such as industrial accidents for fear of legal repercussions.

■ The effect of a law is sometimes to have the reverse effect of that for which it was designed. A good example from the 1970s is where, at a time of high inflation, larger UK manufacturers had to clear their price increases in advance with the Price Commission. This was an extraordinary burden on management time and also on the officials administering the controls, many of whom had limited experience in the matters with which they were dealing. Even some of the toughest buyers in the country accepted prices that had the approval of the Commission, so that the effect of competition was greatly weakened and some manufacturers were even able to widen their margins during this period.

■ Some laws can be so prescriptive that more benefit accrues to the legal profession than is achieved towards the objectives for which the laws were passed in the first place. (This was alleged to be the case in the US as a result of the Superfund and some of that country's other environmental legislation.)

Too much consumer law?

The consumer movement has brought upon business a great deal of additional legislation, much of which was only too necessary because of the failure of some businesses to recognize adequately the reasonable needs of consumers. Such legislation has covered many of the immoral practices which were mentioned in the previous chapter, such as inadequate product safety, poor or misleading labelling and dishonest promotion and pricing methods. However, excessive consumer protection can pile on extra costs to industry and thence to the consumer, which can be especially serious in times of high inflation.

In the 1970s, so influential did campaigners such as Ralph Nader become and so powerful were the legislators, that manufacturers in the US became very wary even to express their reservations about what was going on. At a sectoral business convention in Houston, Texas, in 1977, when inflation and the resulting business problems were biting hard into profits, a visiting British leader from the same industry was given an unscheduled speaking slot immediately before an official of the Federal Trade Commission was due to address the delegates. Aware of the avalanche of legislation for which the FTC was responsible in reaction to Nader and his acolytes, the guest made the following very simple and obvious statement: 'All consumerism, whether it is good or bad, justified or not, is inflationary.' There was a moment of silence and then a burst of applause from all present – except the FTC official.

The effect of law on competition

The law can also have a perverse influence on competition when it is introduced for reasons of conservation or safety. Building regulations can be so strict on matters of public safety that new competitors are dissuaded from entering the market. This is to some extent acceptable in a sector that is notorious for 'cowboy' operators, but potentially good ones can also be excluded. Or, if production of a given commodity is restricted on the grounds of resource conservation, the result can be to keep up prices. This happened with oil in Texas before prices came to be governed by world trends.

Eurosceptics nowadays delight in emphasizing the excessive predilection of Brussels bureaucrats for introducing intrusive regulations in the name of harmonization within the European Union. They are supposed to establish fair competition in the single market, but only too often uneven enforcement between member countries ensures that in practice the playing field is anything but level.

The more imperfect the working of competition in practice, the more people of principle will insist that the law should intervene. Sometimes the outcome can be even worse. Milton Friedman had a good way of putting it: 'Concentrated power [of the state] is not rendered harmless by the good intentions of those who create it.'

Earlier in this chapter it was mentioned that German companies had gained competitive advantage from environmental regulation, but in some ways the opposite has also been the case. Below is an extract from a remarkable speech made in Berlin in April 1997 about Germany's unemployment levels and the nation's need for renewal and social change. It was a heartfelt expression of that typically German (and therefore untranslatable) condition, national *Angst*, and was considered by many commentators to be highly controversial in comparing the situation there to the US:

> Germany is in serious danger of falling behind.
>
> Whoever shows initiative here, and above all whoever wants to strike out in a new direction, is in danger of being suffocated by a mountain of well-meaning regulations. To grasp the extent of the German regulatory mania, one has only to attempt to build an ordinary family house. Although wages are similar in the Netherlands, it is much cheaper to build the same house there, because of Germany's extra costs.
>
> And this bureaucratic mentality doesn't only obstruct anybody who wants to build himself a house; it obstructs entrepreneurs large and small, and most especially it obstructs anyone reckless enough to want to start a business in Germany. Bill Gates started off in a garage and as a young man he found himself running a multinational company. Some say bitterly that here in Germany his garage workshop would have been closed down by the health and safety inspectors.

If these words had been uttered by some obscure commentator, they might have gone unnoticed, but this was not the case. The speaker was no less a person than Roman Herzog, the President of the Federal Republic.

Conclusions on the law in business

The law is essential in such key areas as enforceability of contracts, protection of intellectual property, war against fraud and, above all, prevention of restrictive practices. It should be used selectively in matters relating to the protection of the consumer and the environment, only in exceptional circumstances to limit trade through protectionism, and never to reduce competition through the control of wages and prices.

For all the reasons given above, business prefers to rely heavily on self-regulation, as is argued in the next section, but such reliance is clearly jeopardized every time a self-regulatory regime fails. So often, when this happens, business has only itself to blame.

THE ROLE OF SELF-REGULATION

Advocates of free markets believe in minimum interference by the state and maximum self-regulation within a framework of law. The main justification for this belief is the perception of the weaknesses of the law, as set out above. But self-regulation takes several different forms. It can be external to a profession or company or it can be formulated internally.

The external variety includes the work of generally effective statutory bodies such as the UK Advertising Standards Authority (already described in Chapter 3) and other, less effective, organizations in the financial services sector which are now subsumed into the Financial Services Authority (FSA). (It remains to be seen to what extent self-regulation will be effective in an industry which has been perceived as the subject of too many scandals.)

The second, internal, variety comprises sectoral industry and professional codes and those of individual firms and companies, which have already been quoted extensively in the previous chapters. Both can be national or international in scope, those of multinational companies having great potential in operating across frontiers. Such codes are nothing less than the institutionalization of ethics and are especially useful in those areas which are not (and many would say should not be) taken care of by legislation. They have the advantage over the law in that they can be specifically aimed at the very diverse needs of different professions and different sorts of industries. They are also more flexible than the law and can be changed much more quickly than laws can be amended.

Having listed the weaknesses of the law, it would be unbalanced not to do the same for self-regulation. Its weaknesses include the following:

- A tendency to develop the lowest common denominator acceptable to participants, either in the rules themselves or in conformity with them. This can be a competitive issue, in that companies may be unwilling to put themselves at a disadvantage by going beyond minimum compliance.

- The fact that sanctions against transgressors are usually inadequate. This raises interesting ethical questions as to whether representative trade bodies have the mechanisms to monitor compliance or the will to discipline members, for fear of losing subscriptions.

- The problem that where differing sectors are involved in a single code there can be very different interpretations of what compliance means, because of the wide variety of ways in which each sector is affected.

- The danger of serious confusion about how different codes relate to one another. Some business executives complain that there are actual conflicts between codes and deplore the time needed to check compliance, thus providing lucrative opportunities to armies of consultants.

In spite of these weaknesses of self-regulation, there is a view that business is best changed constructively for the better by itself and its supporters from within, rather than by its critics, some of whom seem to want to prohibit and regulate some businesses into oblivion. This view is only sustainable if the improvements are actually made and are not just window-dressing. Milton Friedman put the point in a sporting context: 'In both games and society, no set of rules can prevail unless most participants, most of the time, conform to them without external sanctions.' In other words, self-regulation works best within some sort of legal framework backed by effective mechanisms for monitoring compliance.

Mention has been made in previous chapters of codes that have been developed for industrial sectors or individual professions. These are important and helpful if companies or professional firms have no codes of their own, but in practice there is no substitute for codes which are company-specific and relevant to each business, whatever its size.

Before codes are developed it is important, if not vital, for a company to decide what values govern the conduct of its business, apart from the achievement of competitiveness and profitability. Shareholder value is one thing, but there are others which matter more.

VALUES COME FIRST

The way in which companies compete is governed by many external factors, apart from the law. In the 1995 report of the Royal Society of Arts (RSA) entitled *Tomorrow's Company* (produced for it by Mark Goyder and others), there was a telling sentence about what were called 'Yesterday's Companies' that cling 'to the notion that the law adequately describes the public acceptability of business conduct'. Indeed the report pointed out that the views of all the main stakeholders – customers, suppliers, employees and investors – play their part, while public opinion, reflected or led by the media and consumer pressure groups, can never be ignored.

This raises an issue that is too seldom recognized by business. It is an integral part of society and its values are both influenced by the world around it and have a great influence on it. Kenneth Adams who, through his work at St George's House, Windsor, and as Industrial Fellow of the Comino Foundation, has made a fundamental contribution to these questions and has been one of the inspirations behind this book, said in a talk in 1997:

> It is important to recognize the widespread influence of business not only on our economic state but also on our moral state... The extent of the business activity and the key role of the market reveal the importance of the part played by those who lead in business nationally and locally in establishing the character of society. This influence spreads far beyond what people normally see as the area of business... The discussion of business ethics has sometimes been confined to the ways in which business operates; we have to emphasize that business influences our values through its actual products and services as well as its way of operating.

This means that business not only has to have values, but has to act on them internally and then articulate them externally.

In an address in 1997 to the Christian Association of Business Executives, which founded the Institute of Business Ethics, Tim Melville-Ross, Director General of the Institute of Directors, put it this way:

> I was and remain a great exponent of the need for a clear vision to be articulated and for a plan to be put in place to achieve that vision... Whatever business is for, I believe it has to operate according to a set of values which most people would regard as acceptable if it has to have any chance of succeeding in its ultimate objective of increasing long term shareholder value.

These ideas go far beyond the more traditional statements of objectives by companies – absolutely valid in themselves – which refer to increasing market share, becoming market leader in a particular field, or achieving a specified return on net assets. Some larger businesses aspire to becoming 'a world class company', a concept that covers a wide range of excellence and nowadays often includes mission statements or declarations of values, placed for all to see in the entrance hall of their imposing offices. Some people may raise their eyebrows cynically, wondering whether such companies are wearing their virtue on their sleeves and whether all this is mere window-dressing without substance.

Some companies indeed take care not to be too outspoken about their virtues, just because such arrogance can invite critics to go out of their way to pick holes in what they do. They prefer their actions to speak for themselves, but still make sure that their values are an integral part of the culture of the company.

Statements of values are difficult to draft because they can seem only too obvious, trite and subjective, like paying lip service to motherhood and apple pie. For example, it is far from easy to establish values that will apply and be acceptable in very different cultural and social conditions, but it must still be done without dilution. The best multinationals confirm that really well thought-out core values *will* travel. One such company in the US includes all the obvious words like honesty, integrity, fairness, trust, teamwork, diversity and good citizenship in its statement of values and ends, significantly, with 'a winning attitude', which means competing successfully while retaining the stated values – which is simply the central theme of this book.

One of the ways in which values of this nature can be promulgated in a company is through codes of practice. Statements of values are not an alternative to codes, nor are codes an adequate substitute for statements of values. In practice, values are a necessary underpinning of codes.

THE ROLE OF COMPANY CODES

It has become more and more widely accepted that, in addition to the law, self-regulation through company codes is not simply valuable but is essential to help companies and individuals of principle as they compete in the marketplace.

Most leading US companies have developed quite elaborate codes of ethics, well ahead of their opposite numbers in the UK and Europe. This has been partly because the concept of business ethics developed earlier in the US and partly because tough legislation on and around the subject of competition were put in place there well ahead of similar action in European countries. Obvious examples are US anti-trust legislation and the Foreign Corrupt Practices Act on bribery. As a result, US company codes contain much material on such matters, which require compliance and are consequently both lengthy and legalistic in tone. Sometimes codes have been drawn up by companies in the US and elsewhere in the aftermath of crises that turned into public relations disasters.

An interesting development in the Far East is the work of the Hong Kong Ethics Development Centre, which was established under the auspices of Hong Kong's Independent Commission against Corruption. In 1995 it drew up a model code which it recommended to local businesses on the following grounds:

> Internally, a Code of Conduct conveys to all staff a clear idea of the accepted conduct for achieving business goals. It also helps maintain consistent standards of

behaviour throughout the company... Externally, adoption of a Code of Conduct enhances a company's reputation for fair and responsible dealing. It also strengthens Hong Kong's reputation as an international business centre where honesty and fair play prevails.

The arguments expressed are fully in line with best practice elsewhere. It would be nice to speculate that such ideas might be brought to bear within China itself as it moves away from its old planned economy, especially now that it has taken control of Hong Kong. If so, it might be able to avoid some of the cruder features of primitive capitalism that are only too prevalent in Russia. As in the West, the Hong Kong document recognizes that some of the obligations of business to society are governed by the law, which is 'a final defence against abuse, such as corruption, fraud and other malpractice', but it goes on to make a strong argument in favour of self-regulation in the form of company codes of conduct.

Wherever companies are in the world, they certainly need to include in their codes of practice the prohibition of activities that are against the law, but they also need to address those aspects of competitive activity that are legal but may not be ethical, or which may at least be out of line with the values established over time by the leaders of the company. This is the essential strength of individual company codes, which by definition must:

- be more relevant to the company and firm than any other code and therefore of most help to the people who work there;

- be a source of guidance and strength to employees and reflect stable values, even though they need to be revised from time to time to take account of changing circumstances;

- act as a check on autocrats in a company, who can only too easily place their subordinates in impossible situations;

- help to protect the public from the activities of very powerful companies;

- help companies avoid actions that can cause lasting damage to their reputation.

SOURCES OF HELP IN DRAWING UP CODES

Codification of this kind by individual firms needs to be consistent with the general codes put out by their particular business sector or profession, these having usually been drawn up by the leading members of that sector or profession in the first place.

Members of the marketing function are logically and inevitably more open to the temptation to indulge in unethical competitive practices than people in other functions in most companies; previous chapters have shown this clearly enough. Yet apart from the more narrowly-based professions of advertising and promotion, which for many years have been well covered by very specific codes, the marketing profession as a whole has been rather slow to address the matter. Some marketers might say that fighting for business in fiercely competitive markets is quite difficult enough without bringing ethics into it. Perhaps it is such people who need help most.

The UK Chartered Institute of Marketing (which has 60,000 members, including many in other countries) is aware of this situation. In 1992 it produced a document, *General Regulations for the Provision of Professional Standards and Disciplinary Procedures*, which included provision for setting up an Ethics Committee to review, expand and amend it as necessary. That Committee reviewed the whole question in 1996, recognizing the key position of the profession of marketing as the major interface between business, customers and the public at large; and in 1997 it completed its *Code of Professional Standards, Ethics and Disciplinary Procedures*, which requires its members to maintain high standards of professionalism and integrity and to recognize their responsibilities to customers, employers, colleagues, fellow marketers and to the public in general. It is thus designed to be helpful to members in their day-to-day work, but adherence to it is also a condition of membership. There is a Disciplinary Committee that considers complaints made under a formal procedure for dealing with cases of professional misconduct. It is understood that a member was suspended soon after the new Code came into force for failing to adhere to it.

Members of any industry or profession can benefit by drawing on the relevant aspects of general codes. For instance, accounting firms' own codes are supported and strengthened by those of their professional bodies, which are in turn reflected in the codes of the International Federation of Accountants (IFAC). Similarly, chemical manufacturers' codes are consistent with the Responsible Care initiatives of the UK Chemical Industries Association (CIA), which reflects and contributes to the work of the European chemical manufacturers association, CEFIC.

This hierarchy of self-supporting codes is mirrored by the advertising industry. Individual advertisers and their agents govern themselves by certain standards as laid down by the Advertising Standards Authority and in other national codes, in line with the work done by the European Advertising Tripartite (EAT). On a world scale, there are the International Chamber of Commerce codes on advertising, promotion, market research, bribery (see Chapter 4) and the environment, which *inter alia* provide invaluable help to developing countries and take account of the international nature of this essential feature of competitiveness.

Since its foundation in 1986, the UK Institute of Business Ethics has devoted a substantial proportion of its resources to the encouragement of company codes of ethics in a series of publications by Simon Webley (listed in the Bibliography), and these are designed to give examples of best practice and to show how codes work. Any company that decides – as they all should – to formulate a code can save many hours of management time by drawing on Webley's Illustrative Code in *Codes of Business Ethics*, published in 1993. In it there are over 60 bullet points that companies should consider for inclusion in their own codes, around half of them relating specifically to how they should compete with one another.

NUMBERS AREN'T EVERYTHING

According to surveys made by the Institute of Business Ethics, in the ten years between 1987 and 1997 the proportion of larger companies in the UK (as listed in *The Times 500*) that had formalized codes of practice rose from 18 to 57 per cent. Even this encouraging increase shows that there is still a long way to go, although this statistic excludes the leading professional firms of accountants and solicitors, a very high proportion of which do already have such codes.

In theory many thousands of smaller firms should have codes as well, but there is an obvious problem here. Many of them compete ethically without a code because their owners or directors have personal values which are easily conveyed to employees because they all know each other well. In plenty of others, the reverse is the case. These can usually get away with much wrongdoing in the short term; the hope is that they will come to recognize that the benefits of ethical behaviour set out in the next chapter can indeed increase their competitiveness.

Certainly, few companies – ethical or not – would regard codes themselves as an element in competitiveness. If that were the case, the proportion of companies having them would increase significantly. Of course, codes are not panaceas and offer no solutions in their own right; indeed, they have their own weaknesses, which include:

- an inability to cover all eventualities;
- the engendering of complacency when the code is a mere rule-book unsupported by matching ethical values;
- the fact that, without proper promulgation, training and supporting management systems, they mean nothing and merely serve as corporate 'fig leaves' that can easily be torn away.

The real test of company codes of practice is to what extent they manage to support individual employees faced with hard choices. In this regard, the quality of existing codes is very varied. This is not merely a matter of presentation (many are still in typescript and hardly look authoritative) but a good number of them are very general in character ('we will conduct our business with integrity') and full of loopholes. The codes of US companies are far more comprehensive and detailed because of US legislation, but possibly too complicated just because there has been an attempt to cater for every eventuality.

Whatever the apparent quality of a code, what matters above all is the extent to which it is promulgated in the company, through the exercise of leadership and example by the chairman, chief executive and other directors, through training, and through a systematic approach to making sure the code is read, understood and followed by employees. As one top executive of an international chemical company said, 'The code is the easy bit.' What follows is much more exacting.

This question is admirably covered in Simon Webley's 1995 publication for the IBE, *Applying Codes of Business Ethics*, which lists 'Twelve Steps for Implementing a Code'. These were seen by *The Financial Times* as such a useful checklist that they were published in full. They are reproduced here at Appendix E. Unless this advice is, and is seen to be, followed, the gap between what business leaders say and what their companies do will not be closed. Codes then risk being condemned as a sham and self-regulation is brought into disrepute.

CONCLUSION AND ADVICE FOR INDIVIDUALS

Individual managers almost invariably consider themselves to be more ethical than their employers. This was confirmed fairly recently by research: the Institute of Management published in 1994 a survey of ethics in management by Stephen Brigley of Bath University under the title *Walking the Tightrope*. In response to questions about the individual and the organization, the (self-selected) respondents not unexpectedly demonstrated a high level of personal ethical awareness but consistently felt that their organizations demonstrated lower standards than their own. In most instances they said they would be willing to 'speak out' (the expression 'whistle-blowing' was not used) if the organization seemed to them to fall short. Resolving the tensions between the individual and the organization on ethical matters, which gave the study its title, was shown to be difficult, particularly when job security was fragile. One manager was quoted as saying: 'High unemployment affects your ethics – cynical but true!'. The survey also made the rather obvious point that the more senior managers were, the easier it was for them to take a stand on ethical matters.

The sort of pontificating that comes from many writers and lecturers on ethics can sound a rather hollow note to people struggling day by day in a harsh competitive climate. The leaders and main supporters of the Institute of Business Ethics are all people who have considerable practical experience of business, either current or recent. Such people understand that when someone is faced with a competitive problem, the decision about the best course of action is likely to be based in the first instance on cost–benefit considerations. Only then might he or she look at some of the longer-term implications, such as the effect on people who might have to be made redundant, the effect on the company's reputation, or the environment, especially if that is not easily measurable on current knowledge. The person of principle, who can take such decisions on his or her personal authority, is fortunate indeed.

The Chartered Institute of Marketing, in its *Guidelines* mentioned earlier, recognizes that members who run their own businesses are in an easier position to abide by the Institute's rules than employees who have to balance morality with career prospects and loyalty to the company, because taking a moral stance can make an individual feel quite lonely. For such employees, a possible support might be the provision of a professional 'helpline' or even a non-attributable advice column in the Institute's magazine, which would also provide a means of spreading best practice among the membership.

Help of this kind can be invaluable when colleagues – or worse, superiors – advocate a course of action that appears to be wrong and so put the individual in a seemingly impossible situation. Apart from anything else, moral questions are far from straightforward and views on the balance between such considerations and the practical implications (which may themselves have moral overtones) place all involved in a veritable minefield. As stated in Chapter 4 a bribe, which is judged essential to gaining a contract for a company otherwise faced with heavy redundancies, must seem to many as less morally reprehensible than the alternative. 'Grey area' problems are only too easily matched by 'grey area' solutions.

In such situations, a properly promulgated company code, which is thoroughly embedded in the organization's culture, is absolutely invaluable in providing the support needed. IBM-UK recognized this specifically in its Conduct Guidelines:

> Normally the law and ethical values coincide. Sometimes, however, an activity may be technically lawful but be unethical or contrary to the Group's standards. If that situation arises, follow the Group's ethical values and standards. The Group's reputation is so important that compliance with the letter of the law is not enough.

Such support is also needed when an individual knows of actions that are clearly wrong being taken by colleagues for the sake of competitiveness. Does that person blow the whistle in the name of his or her own personal integrity, that of someone else, or that of the company? Does that person risk antagonizing colleagues by doing so or worse, risk losing a valuable well-paid job and jeopardizing the security of his or her family?

'Whistle-blowing' is an expression often loosely used by the media, but it is only a very negative recourse of last resort, usually when the misdeed has taken place. It is not a good way of describing the facility that should be available to employees as part of the culture of a well-run company or firm. Employees need to know where they can obtain advice and help without prejudice to their jobs to try and *prevent* something being done that is thought to be in breach of a code. Some companies have 'hotlines' for this purpose, which enable employees, anonymously in some cases, to contact someone separate from their own area of work. (For example, Diageo's Minneapolis-based food company Pillsbury has a freephone 'In Touch' line, which enables employees to telephone anonymously to notify management of issues of concern.) There is always the danger of mischief-making when providing such a service, but that is a risk that should be worth taking.

Ultimately the proof of the pudding is in the eating. Companies need to value and expect loyalty from employees, but not in all circumstances. Of course unprincipled employees can be loyal to an unethical company – the Artful Dodger was loyal to Fagin. But in most circumstances companies must earn the loyalty of employees of integrity and not make life difficult for them by placing them in compromising situations. It should certainly be unnecessary for employees to rely on external legal protection for whistle-blowing, for example. Not for nothing does the IBE's *Illustrative Code* recommend that the company should aim 'to create the climate and opportunities for employees to voice genuinely held concerns about behaviour or decisions that they perceive to be unethical'.

Macchiavelli, in *The Prince*, argued that there was one rule for business and another for private life. Only too many people in business subscribe to this idea as some sort of justification for moral turpitude in the marketplace. As T L Beauchamp argued in *Ethical Theory and Business*, there is a hierarchy of *principles*, *rules* and *judgments* on how competition should be conducted: competition should be fair and based on moral *principles*; there should be *rules* to translate these principles into practice, through the law and through voluntary restraint; and *judgments* must be made about what to do in particular instances. It is here that corporate values and personal consciences come into play.

The ideal situation is for the individual with a conscience to recognize the principles and apply the rules without hesitation and fear of criticism from colleagues or superiors. But there must always be issues where personal principles on how to compete in an ethical manner must prevail, whatever personal risks are involved. As Charles Handy said in one of his memorable *Thought for the Day* broadcasts: 'You can't delegate your conscience to keep your soul intact.'

Chapter 7

Ethical behaviour and competitive edge

Why is business so often on the defensive about ethics? Part of the answer is that unethical behaviour makes good copy: routine good behaviour is only too often dull. Too much of the discussion on ethics in competition is negative, of the 'thou shalt not' variety. Chapters 3–5 of this book are no exception.

Yet the refusal to adopt the unethical practices mentioned in those chapters can in itself have a positive outcome. Michael Novak in *Business is a Calling* cites the chief executive who takes the line that 'there are certain things this firm will never do' and sticks to them. To apply such principles in competition can lose business in the short term and can affect profits because, as he says, 'high moral standards incur costs'. Yet those same standards 'sometimes turn out to be, especially over time, a competitive advantage'. Warren Kingston in *Ethics the Only Win–Win Strategy for Business* makes the point in this way: 'Ethics is about winning in the long term. Good business and good ethics are not a contradiction in terms.'

The Hong Kong Ethics Development Centre document mentioned in the previous chapter is very clear on this: 'Business ethics,' it states, 'is good business. It makes for better staff and a more valuable goodwill, which all goes to strengthening the company's competitive edge in the long run.' This is what this chapter is all about.

The CBI's 1973 Watkinson Report stressed that 'mere compliance with the law does not necessarily make a good citizen or a good company' and that 'moral imperatives' should not enter the culture of a firm from Companies Acts but from within. This idea had been embraced particularly in relation to the environment, as will be shown later in this chapter, but it has far wider implications. The RSA's *Tomorrow's Company* report says that 'business leaders must develop a new language of business success'.

RESERVATIONS ON AN ETHICAL APPROACH

These ideas are questioned by sceptics, because many companies get away with acting immorally, at least in the short term. Hard-headed go-getters can push companies with 'fuzzy ideas' out of existence. Others point out that the more competition there is, the fewer opportunities there are for doing good for society as opposed to improving returns for shareholders.

Professor Norman Barry of the University of Buckingham says that social responsibility is popular because 'it is easier to do good than ensure maximum returns for stockholders' and argues that the more time and resource a company puts into social responsibility, the more likely it is to be taken over. (It is true that some of the expenditure associated with corporate social responsibility and worthy causes – especially those personal to the chairman and his colleagues – are the first to be cut out after a takeover.) There is no denying that the disbursement of discretionary funds increases the feel-good factor of the directors and managers responsible, and purists can rightly point out that this in itself diminishes the ethical value of their 'generosity'.

Theodore Levitt in *The Dangers of Social Responsibility* regarded such activities as 'peripheral' to businesses, which should be 'concentrating in fighting each other in the market place... In the end,' he wrote, 'business has only two responsibilities – to obey the elementary canons of everyday face-to-face civility (honesty, good faith and so on) and seek material gain'. Levitt was also concerned that excessive involvement in society would get companies too far embroiled in the proper responsibilities of government. Here he had a point: the keenness of many governments to curb public expenditure has led them to try to get business to foot the bill directly for more and more activities that should be funded out of taxation.

Hard-nosed reservations of this kind would seem to be receding nowadays, but there does remain a problem for even the most socially responsible businesses in times of recession and increased competition: the difficulty of measuring the benefits of their social programmes when many of the costs, in terms of budgets and management time, are much more visible. Because of this, the growing army of proponents of higher standards of business ethics all agree that they must provide more case examples to demonstrate the benefits that good behaviour brings to the bottom line if they are to counter these understandable reservations.

This chapter includes examples from several countries where excellent work is described that has undoubtedly enhanced the company's reputation. Such work often involves measurable short-term costs, but the benefits are hard to evaluate and are by their very nature long-term. The point here is that such benefits are recognized as being without price.

It should be remembered that the ultimate profitability of a company is determined by many other external and internal factors apart from how ethically it competes. For example, there are many companies (some of which are mentioned in this book) that have excellent ethical track records, but for quite different reasons have still not performed very well financially. This does not necessarily prove the points made by the sceptics quoted above: if these companies had not competed so ethically, they might well have performed even worse than they did.

So, whatever the reservations may be, the purpose of this chapter is to look positively at how ethical behaviour in competition and a due sense of respect for all stakeholders can actually give a company competitive advantage. It is obvious that it is preferable to do business with people one can trust rather than with crooks, but a company cannot establish a reputation for trustworthiness, integrity and appropriate social responsibility overnight; it requires a long term, strategic approach.

TAKING THE LONGER-TERM VIEW IN THE INTERESTS OF ALL STAKEHOLDERS

Will Hutton, in *The State We're In*, is highly critical of the alleged pursuit of short-term profits by investors in UK companies, in contrast to the longer-term attitude taken by banks investing in German companies and the elaborate cross-shareholdings of the larger Japanese industrial and trading groups. He blames 'footloose institutional shareholders and boards alike' in demanding 'business strategies that boost the short-term share price'. It is not just short-term profits that come in for such criticism but the proportion of earnings that is paid out in dividends, compared with the amount retained for research and development and for investment in the future of the business.

Hutton's arguments were refuted robustly in 1996 by the National Association of Pension Funds in a pamphlet entitled *Good Corporate Governance*, which made many of the points that are the subject of this chapter and which asserted that 'contrary to popular mythology, pension funds are already "patient investors" '.

Some readers might anyway question whether short-termism is strictly speaking a practical rather than an ethical issue. Maximization of short-term profits can be a question of survival for a small firm, while larger firms with significant market share can take a more relaxed, longer-term view. Foregoing immediate profitability may be made out to stem from altruism, but can pay off in terms of longer-term profitability and, as argued previously, less easily measured benefits to company reputation. Indeed, although companies may be able to profit in the short term by competing unethically, subsequent sections in this chapter will try and show that principles and profit are not merely compatible in the longer term but depend upon each other.

The President of Quantum Chemical Corporation of the US, John H Stookey, summed up the point well when he said that 'ethical issues come down to the fundamental question of how much of today's benefit you are willing to forego for tomorrow's gain'. The RSA's *Tomorrow's Company* report makes the point in this way: 'The companies which will sustain competitive success in the future are those which focus less exclusively on shareholders and on financial measures of success – and instead include all their stakeholder relationships, and a broader range of measurements, in the way they think about their purpose and performance.'

The emphasis is that there should be 'reciprocal relationships' with all stakeholders. In an article in *The Times* in May 1996, Lord Alexander, Chairman of NatWest, wrote:

> ... the stakeholder approach, in reality, reminds us of what we should have known, and been doing, all along. A company that wants to have a long-term and profitable future must earn and retain the confidence of shareholders, customers, staff, suppliers and the wider community. As much as anything else, the stakeholder approach reminds us of what is needed for long-term financial success. And it is consistent with the view that the prime duty of managers is to deliver long-term value to shareholders.

The stakeholder concept, which has already been mentioned many times in this book, came very much into fashion in the 1990s, but one of its inspirations was the thinking behind George Goyder's book, *The Responsible Company*, published in 1959, which he followed 18 years later with *The Just Enterprise*, both being based on a lifetime's experience in business, with a spell in government service during the Second World War.

Within companies acknowledging the stakeholder concept, there are very different views about which are the most important. It is natural for marketing and sales people to put customers first, while the buying department favours suppliers, the trades union representatives favour employees and the accountants' devotion to the bottom line, by implication, favours shareholders. The chairman (or his wife) may be one of the few who regard society outside the company as important, although others may well have interests as school governors, magistrates, or members of local organizations.

The concept that the planet itself and future generations are also stakeholders began to emerge in the 1970s. Even the most far-sighted business people found it very difficult to accept this concept, but by the 1990s sustainable development had become more than a catch-all slogan.

The next section of this chapter deals briefly with each of these points, deliberately leaving investors to the last, but after that adding the need to check on what is done and report accordingly. The topics covered are:

- integration with the community

- respecting the environment and striving for sustainability

- treating suppliers as partners

- regarding service to customers as paramount

- treating employees as the most valuable asset

- attracting investors

- ethical auditing and reporting.

INTEGRATION WITH THE COMMUNITY

Is corporate social responsibility only the avoidance of unethical practices of the sort mentioned in previous chapters, maybe with some charitable giving thrown in? Community involvement in the wider sense was practised by some companies long before George Goyder's time. For example, the Quaker chocolate companies, Cadbury, Rowntree and Fry, did well in business because of a combination of good products, honest dealing and social responsibility. It was especially appropriate that the first of these names became associated with more recent thinking on corporate governance.

Acting as good corporate citizens

Ever since the Watkinson Report was published in 1973, the idea has developed that business has a responsibility to the immediate community around it and that the larger companies have moral obligations to the nation as a whole. Indeed, Watkinson specifically said that a company should act 'as a good citizen in business'.

This is in stark contrast to the ideas of Milton Friedman – as expressed in *Capitalism and Freedom*, quoted in Chapter 1 – who believed the social responsibility of business was simply to maximize profits. He regarded corporate social responsibility as a 'subversive doctrine' and 'pure and unadulterated socialism', on the grounds that such activities were outside the remit of companies and were the moral responsibility of shareholders.

Friedman was mainly referring to a very narrow form of social responsibility, namely financial contributions to good causes – an attitude shared by a nowadays diminishing number of well known business leaders. The argument from some of them that this responsibility should be left to shareholders is unsound anyway, because of the growing importance of institutional shareholders, which are in turn responsible to their clients, including pensioners, and are therefore prevented from fulfilling this role.

Whatever companies' policies are in relation to the community, critics will cynically dismiss the whole exercise as an elaborate, guilt-driven means of trying to ensure public acceptance of their activities or even of their very existence, and may even dare to sneer at an organization such as Business in the Community (BitC). However, it is inconceivable that the 400-odd companies that support it can all be regarded as soft do-gooders. They believe it is right to raise the quality and extent of their involvement in the community, which brings them nearer to the customers they serve and is thus an indirect, but not necessarily insignificant, way of improving competitiveness. In other words, there are good business reasons for doing so rather than just the need to follow a whim of the chairman's wife.

A prominent supporter of BitC is Grand Metropolitan, the international food and drinks company which has now merged with Guinness to form the Diageo group. GrandMet's Annual Report for 1996 stated that its 'definition of success goes beyond earnings growth and a strong balance sheet'. It acknowledged that lasting commercial success depended not only on stable markets, highly skilled and motivated employees and prosperous consumers, but also on 'healthy communities'. It said that 'community involvement is a vital part of corporate citizenship because it is proactive. It shows that the company is not content just to comply with high standards of behaviour; we also want to contribute actively to the community.'

GrandMet's *Report on Corporate Citizenship* of 1997 had some interesting examples of these principles put into practice in the US, the UK, India and South Africa. For example, in the US its Heublein Inc, which produces, imports and markets spirits and wines, 'moved its 425 corporate headquarters staff in March 1996 from the affluent suburb of Farmington, Connecticut, into the heart of Hartford, one of the most impoverished cities in the US' and received, they claimed, 'a hero's welcome'. The move came less than a year after Heublein's decision to close its Hartford manufacturing plant, so they owed something anyway to the already depressed city of 130,000 inhabitants. In addition, the company contributed to inner-city renewal by supporting struggling restaurants, local arts groups and sports events. Quite rightly, these activities were a source of pride for their employees and were not totally isolated from increased demand for the company's products. Even before he could assess the full impact of these programmes, Hartford's Mayor, Michael J Peters, said that Heublein had already been a key driver in the city's economic recovery.

Charitable donations

Charitable donations by businesses are lower in the UK than in the US, with only very few companies giving away as much as three per cent of profits and the majority well under one per cent. Some of this giving could be considered to be completely altruistic, with no visible benefit to the company, but some companies quite understandably prefer to support causes that are in some way relevant to the company, such as, for example, the provision of computers and proprietary software for schools or the gift of four-wheel-drive vehicles to deliver food aid over difficult terrain in the third world.

For example, one of the UK's leading companies, British Telecom (BT), believing as they do that 'successful companies need successful communities', is active in raising standards in schools to help pupils and their teachers to benefit from new communications technologies. Following pilot schemes at a small number of schools where BT provided initial training and ongoing support involving fax, telephone, e-mail, the Internet and video-conferencing, the project is being extended to schools in different parts of the UK. At one school in Scotland, the French class is linked with schoolchildren in France and other pupils in Britain who are also learning French.

Cause-related marketing

A growing method for linking charitable giving with the enhancement of company image is 'cause-related marketing' (CRM), which is promoted in the UK by Business in the Community. They describe this as 'a commercial activity by which a company with an image, product or service to market builds a relationship with a cause or a number of causes for mutual benefit. It is nothing more than enlightened self-interest.' The idea is that a company can promote itself or its products to the public through external activities, promising that a proportion of the profits will be given to a specified charity or cause. For example, to support the fiftieth anniversary of the United Nations Children's Fund (UNICEF), British Petroleum donated 70 UK pence for every copy produced of their 1996 calendar. The theme of the calendar was 'Working together for a better world' and it featured people and environments where both BP and UNICEF were involved. The calendar was enthusiastically received, 17,000 were printed and copies were distributed in 20 countries.

A second example can be gleaned from an entirely different company in the UK. Cadbury Ltd, the chocolate-products arm of the Cadbury Schweppes group, sponsored 31 pantomimes across the UK over six years in aid of the international charity Save the Children (SCF). Their objectives were simple: to enhance Cadbury's image of being fun, contemporary and caring; to reinforce their corporate values, especially to families with children; and to raise funds for the SCF. The company achieved significant media exposure and a high profile before an annual audience of 1.75 million, and £200,000 was raised for the SCF in three seasons alone.

Research commissioned by BitC in 1996 and 1997 shows that this technique not only benefits the companies and the causes in the obvious ways, but is viewed very positively by consumers. Not only do they expect large businesses to demonstrate active social responsibility and approve of this way of doing it, but they also see it as an easy way for them to contribute indirectly to such causes.

EMPLOYEE INVOLVEMENT

There are other companies which believe that they can show their sense of responsibility by seconding their own people to work in the community.

One of these takes quite a hard-headed view of responsibility to the community and does indeed regard it as good for business. Sir Richard Greenbury, Chairman of Marks & Spencer, is quoted as believing that the company, as a retailer, needs a healthy community in which to grow and prosper. This is the basis of its policy of social spending and its becoming a founder member of Business in the Community. For example, it seconds managers to outside activities such as youth work, crime reduction and environmental improvement, which is good for both the personal development of the secondees and for the reputation of the company. It believes its people carry with them the company's culture and values wherever they go. The 1996 Annual Report contained a section on social responsibility entitled 'Marks & Spencer at the heart of the community', with two pages of information on the implementation of its social and environmental policies. The same pattern was repeated a year later.

Protecting human rights

The examples of good citizenship mentioned so far are simple enough, but the idea that business is an integral part of society can raise some very big issues indeed. For instance, does the role of business in the community include a responsibility for helping to protect human rights? Traditionally this was regarded as a political issue best left in the hands of governments or, if they failed in their responsibilities, it was up to NGOs such as Amnesty International to play their part. Indeed, in the past, multinational companies regarded their responsibilities for this issue as applying to their relations with their employees and were careful to avoid appearing to interfere with host governments over infringements of human rights in society as a whole. If they had, they feared that they would be accused by critics of trying to exercise excessive power.

Yet the more business is regarded as part of 'society', which it undoubtedly is, the more there is pressure on multinationals to try to influence governments of countries where human rights are abused, thus drawing them into the political arena. If they do not do so, they are too easily accused of colluding with the régime in power. They can be subjected to the demand to withdraw from such countries, which, where large investments in plant and people are involved, is easier said than done. The question then arises as to whether it is better for the employees, the customers, the suppliers and the local community if the company stays. Besides, régimes or governments change, maybe for the better in part because of the good influence of large, responsible international companies in their midst alongside local entrepreneurs with lower standards.

One example of this dilemma is the pressure that there used to be on Western companies to pull out of South Africa under apartheid, which understandably aroused great passions. Some companies bowed to the pressures and withdrew, while others decided to stay put and were derided for supporting the South African régime. World-class companies that decided to stay were often as opposed to apartheid as their critics, but they argued that their superior employment conditions favoured their employees, who would be much worse off if the companies walked away. There is anecdotal evidence that some of the activists against apartheid in the country were privately encouraging the best companies to stay on, knowing that they would be essential to the well-being of the country in the future and recognizing that, in the meantime, their employment practices were helping to undermine the old régime.

More recently Shell, one of the companies which elected to stay in South Africa under apartheid, has been accused of conniving in abuses of human rights in Nigeria and has been put under pressure from activists to withdraw from the country. The issues involved are very complex, and this is not the place to discuss them, but suffice it to say that Shell has refused to give way to that pressure, while admitting that it does have responsibilities in this area. The latest version of its *Statement of General Business Principles*, published in 1997 and reproduced as Appendix F, includes references not only to the human rights of employees but also a commitment 'to conduct business as responsible corporate members of society, to observe the laws of the countries in which they operate, [and] to express support for fundamental human rights in line with the legitimate role of business...'

In the same document, under the heading of Political Activities, it says that 'when dealing with governments Shell companies have the right and the responsibility to make their position known on any matter which affects themselves, their employees, their customers, or their shareholders. They also have the right to make their position known on matters affecting the community where they have a contribution to make.' Shell is not alone. Rio Tinto (formerly RTZ) gives special attention to this in *The Way We Work*, its 1998 statement of business practice.

Human rights are indeed an important ethical issue, but what have they to do with competition? The answer is that companies that handle these difficult questions more competently than their competitors deserve to win. To be sure, when a company gets into difficulties over these or any other matter of this kind, its competitors say to themselves: 'There but for the grace of God...' In short, companies with vision and values recognize that they are part of the community in a way that goes far beyond the activities within their plants and their offices. In a speech in June 1997, BP's Group Chief Executive, John Browne, said: 'We

116

can't put up the barricades and try to hide from the concerns of society. We're part of that society – not least because our staff have views and opinions of their own which inevitably reflect the wider concerns of society.'

Such companies make sure that they do indeed compete in the marketplace in a responsible way, adopting the practices discussed in the sections below. Moreover, the individuals in these companies have an additional (some would say awesome) responsibility, namely to demonstrate in the way they behave that theirs is an honourable calling and as valuable as it is to be a doctor, a nurse or even a priest. Interestingly, a very senior executive from one highly reputable company found this statement to be 'a bit over the top', thus confirming that the point still needs to be made strongly that the more business people regard their profession as a vocation and behave accordingly, the better they will be respected by society.

RESPECTING THE ENVIRONMENT AND STRIVING FOR SUSTAINABILITY

'We destroy the beauty of the countryside because the unappropriated splendours of nature have no economic value.' Such a view would be deemed commonplace in the last decade of the twentieth century, but it was in fact a visionary statement of John Maynard Keynes over 60 years before the 1992 Rio Earth Summit. It is the basis for the work of environmental economists in costing the damage wrought by business activities.

Regulations to redress the balance have increased exponentially since the 1970s, but there was still plenty of scope for unethical companies to try to gain short-term advantage over their more principled and strategically driven competitors by holding back on often expensive investments that would help protect and sustain the environment.

From the early 1970s the larger (and more vulnerable) companies recognized the importance of developing responsible environmental management techniques. At first they were essentially defensive in nature, but by degrees far-sighted companies recognized that good environmental performance had become a key competitive issue with very long-term strategic implications.

Of all the stakeholders that responsible companies now recognize, the newest and conceptually by far the most difficult for which to accept responsibility are future generations. The day that the memoranda and articles of association of companies include that grouping alongside shareholders is indeed far off. Yet that is what sustainable development is all about.

The most commonly used definition of sustainable development was popularized by *Our Common Future*, the landmark Brundtland Report, published in 1987:

> To ensure that it meets the needs of the present without compromising the ability of future generations to meet their own needs.

In other words, we have no right to plunder the planet in terms of resources and environmental degradation at the expense of future generations. A simple enough concept, but heavily criticized by some people as far too imprecise. It has become at the same time a symbol, an article of faith and a cliché; it is both extremely simple and highly esoteric; and it is bandied about by people with completely opposing views. Frances Cairncross of *The Economist*, in her book *Costing the Earth*, wrote: 'Every environmentally-aware politician is in favour of it, a sure sign that they do not understand what it means.'

But this definition does have advantages. It has brought people of widely differing persuasions to the same table. It also appeals to countries in every stage of development, from the richest to the poorest. Its appeal to international business is that it embraces a new approach to stewardship for the earth and an acknowledgment that economic growth is still necessary. Only such growth, so the argument goes, can create the capacity within industry and the wealth needed by society to solve environmental problems, through fundamental technological breakthroughs in industrial products and processes and new ways of both saving and producing energy.

Striving for sustainable development and competing with other companies to achieve it make demands that pose serious moral and strategic challenges. So far, most companies are active at two much less demanding stages of environmental policy, which are:

- compliance and cost saving;
- compliance-plus and licence to operate.

These terms are discussed further below.

Compliance and cost saving

So far, most environmental improvement has been achieved for reasons of prudence and normal, sound business practice. Firstly, it has been a question of compliance with the increasing body of regulation and the avoidance of fines or more serious penalties. Secondly, it has involved sensible measures, which may in many cases have been presented as moral stewardship for the environment, but which at the same time amounted to improving competitiveness through cost savings, including waste reduction and savings in materials, water and energy.

This came out clearly when the Institute of Business Ethics published a study in 1995 by Hill, Marshall and Priddey entitled *Benefiting Business and the Environment*, which specifically sought to demonstrate, through case studies, that environmental issues were not just a threat and a source of additional cost, but also an opportunity to improve competitiveness. The majority of these examples related to relatively simple measures, mainly instances of routine good management and some of which may have been inspired by environmental concerns, while others were conveniently claimed as such. Some involved no investment, while most of the others required quite small amounts with very rapid payback in one or two years only.

An example quoted in the IBE book was from the UK subsidiary of a Japanese Multinational, Nissan. Some of their model range at the time included high-density polyethylene fuel tanks incorporating nylon linings, which were expensive to make because the unavoidable off-cuts amounted to roughly 30 to 40 per cent of the total weight of material used. Unfortunately, it was considered that the off-cuts could not be recycled because of contamination by the nylon element in them, so they were sent to landfill, which was both costly and environmentally undesirable. However a technology was devised to overcome the problem by granulating the offcuts, making them into pellets, and then mixing them with virgin material to an extent that did not compromise the integrity of the product. In 1993 alone, over £700,000 was saved in raw materials and the capital investment involved was recouped in fifteen months.

But there was a further advantage to the environment, in that company policy allowed them to set off such savings against other improvements, which could never pay for themselves. The plastic offcut recycling enabled Nissan to switch to water-based paints on one model, which in turn helped to reduce solvent emissions.

This is a good example of practical good management and an active environmental policy working together. Another example from the same IBE book comes from the UK subsidiary of a US multinational, Procter & Gamble, which had already developed an environmental policy in the late 1960s and coined the phrase 'more from less' to describe its approach to looking at the environmental effects of its products. In 1990 Procter & Gamble 'reformulated Ariel detergent to produce a more concentrated product, using 30 per cent less ingredients by changing the product formula, but achieving results as good, if not better'. The savings in materials were matched by a similar percentage in packaging, on top of which transport costs were reduced. The company saw further marketing and environmental opportunities of selling liquid and powder detergents in refill containers, and competitors followed their lead.

Examples such as these may be described as relatively soft options, but should not be dismissed as unimportant in themselves, given the prodigality and waste that is the hallmark of so-called advanced countries and the environmental necessity for continued improvement at this level. In fact companies such as those quoted are fully aware that they need to consider longer-term investment for environmental improvement, accepting a payback over longer periods.

Compliance-plus and licence to operate

The next level of environmental stewardship, which has been adopted by most of the larger and more vulnerable companies in such industries as chemicals and energy, is to adopt policies that go well beyond what the law demands. Such policies, which obviously often involve some sacrifice of short-term profitability and can therefore be seen as ethical, also frequently anticipate future legislation, and this may, as has been stated earlier, in turn give a company a strong competitive advantage over those who leave it to the last minute to adjust their practices to new laws.

In other instances, companies hope that by voluntarily committing themselves to continuous environmental improvement they will achieve a 'licence to operate' in the eyes of the public and governments and even succeed in staving off excessive, prescriptive legislation, as discussed in the previous chapter. It is to these ends that the North American and European chemical industries adopted their 'Responsible Care' initiatives.

The same motivation led the International Chamber of Commerce (ICC) to draw up its *Business Charter for Sustainable Development*, subtitled *Principles for Environmental Management*, in 1991 in anticipation of the Rio Earth Summit (UNCED) the following year. This statement of principles (there are sixteen of them) covered all the steps needed to establish policies, management systems and necessary reporting which were, and still are, seen as essential to companies of all sizes in all sorts of industries, including the service industries, in countries all over the world. In the UK itself, the *Business Charter* was taken up by the CBI in its Environmental Forum and reflected in other initiatives such as Business in the Environment.

The common theme of all these activities is to persuade companies on both moral and practical grounds to do much more about environmental improvement than the law required and to regard such work as highly desirable, if not essential, in competitive terms.

Moving towards sustainability

A third stage is urged more and more by environmental campaigners, many of whom reluctantly give business some credit for achievements in the first two stages while rightly pointing out that far more small and medium-sized companies (SMEs) need to be got on board. They say that the ICC *Business Charter* was still much more about environmental management (as shown in its subtitle), but that it does not live up to the implications of its main title (which included the words 'Sustainable Development') as defined by Brundtland.

So far there are not many examples of companies seriously addressing these issues in practice, although many of the best ones are thinking about it. For example, companies in the energy field, whether it be from coal, oil, gas or electricity, are forced to consider both the possible (environmentalists say certain) threat of climate change (already touched on in Chapter 5) and the dwindling supplies of their raw materials and are therefore thinking about what business they will be in in 20 or 30 years' time.

By the very nature of their business, oil companies plan further ahead than most. Shell is not alone in recognizing the need to seek alternative sources of energy and has even built it into its revised *Statement of General Business Principles* (see Appendix F). There it states 'The objectives of Shell companies are to engage efficiently, responsibly and profitably in the oil, gas, chemicals and other selected businesses and to participate in the search for and development of other sources of energy.' Towards the end of 1997 the Shell group established a fifth core business, Shell International Renewables (SIR), which initially aimed to invest more than half a billion US dollars in renewables, mainly biomass and photovoltaic sources. The stated aim is to capture a ten per cent share of this one-billion-dollar rapidly-expanding market before 2005. Surprisingly (yet encouragingly), the group estimates that renewable energy sources could satisfy half the world's energy requirements by 2050.

In similar vein, BP's John Browne said in the speech quoted earlier:

> ... we can also be part of the solution by developing the technologies which add to the world's energy supply without adding to emissions. That's why we're now developing our solar business, which has been in existence for the last fifteen years. Solar isn't yet commercially competitive with other sources of power generation, but we think that, given the right support and incentives, it could be competitive in supplying peak load capacity in the next ten to fifteen years.

Another company faced with quite a different resource problem and which is giving it thought is Unilever. Sustainable development issues are recognized at the most senior levels in that company as a corporate priority because they have a direct bearing in its long-term business success. The recognition of the crisis in global fish stocks has led the company to set up the Marine Stewardship Council (MSC) together with the World Wide Fund for Nature (WWF). The Council is an independent, non-profit, non-governmental body that has established a broad set of principles for sustainable fishing and set standards for individual fisheries. Products from fisheries certified to MSC standards are marked with an on-pack logo, so allowing consumers to select fish products from sustainable, well managed sources.

International business has for a very long time argued that industrial activity that the critics see as the problem can also, as John Browne of BP said in his speech, be the source of solutions that would achieve more for the environment through technological innovation than lawmakers could ever do. This point has already been made in the previous chapter but needs to be repeated here. In 1989, Peter Wallenberg, the Swedish industrialist who was the ICC's World

President at that time, wrote: 'The onus of proving that sustainable development is feasible rests primarily on the private business sector, as it controls most of the technological and productive capacity needed to conceive more environmentally benign processes, products and services and to introduce them throughout the world.'

In 1991 in preparation for the Rio summit, Stephan Schmidheiny, the Swiss businessman who set up the Business Council for Sustainable Development in 1991 (now called the World Business Council for Sustainable Development and based in Geneva) published a book entitled *Changing Course*. He is reported to have said recently: 'a lot more can be done if more businesses view the environment as an innovation challenge rather than a compliance cost.' This reflects the work that is being done by oil companies to develop new energy sources to replace fossil fuels and car makers to work on more environmentally friendly ways of propelling vehicles than the internal combustion engine. Indeed, Ford is reported to have announced in late 1997 that it had come together with Daimler-Benz to develop vehicles to be propelled by environmentally friendly fuel cells. Developed by Ballard Power Systems of Canada, these fuel cells had already been used in space missions and could be included in a commercially viable vehicle by 2004.

Of course industry alone cannot, and should not, be expected to deliver sustainable development. Yet the prizes to companies which succeed in achieving breakthroughs of this kind in competition with each other will be tremendous and matched by the benefits to the environment. There is no better example of how competition and ethics can come together.

TREATING SUPPLIERS AS PARTNERS

In a fiercely competitive marketplace, it would seem normal to most buyers to adopt at all times a detached stance, so that the best possible terms of quality, delivery, service and price are squeezed from suppliers. That is the buyer's job, but not if a valued supplier is put out of business as a result and there is no obvious alternative.

In Chapter 5 there was discussion of unethical practices in relation to suppliers, these matters not always being covered by codes of practice. However some companies explicitly declare that they regard their suppliers as partners. One retailer, Safeway, spells this out in a most businesslike way: 'We work in partnership with our suppliers... while we will be exacting customers, we will be fair in all our dealings. We aim to develop long-term relationships of mutual respect and understanding with our suppliers and trading partners.'

In a document entitled *The Purpose and the Role*, another retailer, W H Smith, emphasizes the long-term relationship as follows: 'We will aim to forge a lasting link, developing a relationship from which both sides will prosper. We should always treat our suppliers fairly and expect high standards from them in return.' In similar fashion, Boots emphasizes the importance of treating smaller suppliers fairly: 'It is the policy of the Company to ensure that. . . there is no abuse of economic power in dealing with a smaller concern.' And one of the larger retailers, Marks & Spencer, is so confident of its collaboration with suppliers and all other aspects of its company ethos that it does not have a written code at all. Asked about this, one buyer said: 'M&S does not buy products off the shelf. They are engineered in partnership with suppliers. This gives us a real competitive edge on retailers which buy at arms length.'

Most industrial buyers' references to suppliers are those that specifically forbid receiving inducements from them, but Ford, one of the toughest of buyers, refers specifically to its suppliers as 'our partners'. Another large industrial company, British Gas, published its *Principles* in 1992, committing itself to 'showing understanding of [the suppliers'] problems and challenges and... developing mutual respect notwithstanding the continuation of keen commercial negotiations'.

Nowhere are the ethical aspects of buyer–supplier relationships more sensitive than when the buyer is in a developed country and the supplier is in one of the poorer countries in the third world. Traidcraft is a company that imports from poor countries under carefully stated rules based on the Christian principles of justice and concern for others. It is a supporter of the UK Ethical Trading Initiative, which was launched in 1998. Traidcraft and other supporters, including major supermarket chains, believe in avoiding exploitation of people, especially children, and ensuring that the goods they purchase are produced in conditions that are safe and decent and provide a reasonable living to the people who produce them. These aims are supported by codes of conduct.

These examples of intent, providing they are followed in practice, show how many companies believe that a responsible attitude to their suppliers as partners is a valuable aspect of their own long-term competitiveness.

REGARDING SERVICE TO CUSTOMERS AS PARAMOUNT

Whether in manufacturing or services, businesses can be said to have two aspects: the mechanical, represented by production, research, purchasing and accounting functions; and service, represented by sales, distribution and marketing. Those production departments that are indifferent to and isolated from customer needs (as in the former Soviet Union and only too many UK companies up to the 1970s – and some even today) are in the last analysis only concerned about how much is produced. However, people involved in research and product development who are not prepared to be influenced by market needs should not be in industry at all. The service ethic is essential to competitiveness and the idea of service is where ethics and business can come most closely together.

There are three aspects to regarding customer service as paramount. Firstly, service to customers and getting close to them is itself a highly ethical activity. Secondly, it is one of the paramount ingredients of excellence in management – one of the 'eight basics' which were identified by Peters and Waterman in their book, *In Search of Excellence*. (Some of the companies quoted in that book may not look quite so healthy now, but this should not be allowed to weaken this aspect of their case.) Thirdly, customers are more and more inclined, all other things being more or less equal, to buy from companies that are seen to be ethical. Below, the first two are combined in one section and the third has a section of its own.

Service to customers is both ethical and fundamental to good business

This statement seems so obvious to anyone who has been involved with sales and marketing that it hardly seems worth saying, yet there are still product-orientated companies in manufacturing and services that do not see this, or that only pay lip service to the idea, without putting it into practice. These are the companies, as Peters and Waterman put it, that either ignore customers or consider them 'a bloody nuisance'. On the other hand, they say, the commitment to service to customers starts with the company's philosophy, is thus embedded in its values and is exercised by senior executives through personal example. A simple instance is an Aer Lingus advertisement: 'We don't just fly planes, we fly people.'

Such companies put service before profit, because they know that profit will follow naturally. Some of them take the view that *everyone* in the firm, regardless of the job they do, is involved in some way in selling, not just the obvious people like receptionists and switchboard operators. Associate that idea with providing value to the customer and we have a powerful ethical concept which is essential to competitiveness.

Asda, the supermarket chain, nearly went under in the early 1990s. Its truly remarkable recovery under its Chairman, Patrick Gillam and its Chief Executive, Archie Norman (who subsequently succeeded Gillam as Chairman), is ideal raw material for management textbooks. One of their published core values is that 'selling is a universal responsibility'. Another is: 'what we sell will be better value because we are totally committed to value; that is part of the ethic.'

Associated with service are the equally moral principles of quality and reliability. Peters and Waterman single out Caterpillar as a 'superb example':

Caterpillar offers customers 48-hour guaranteed parts delivery service anywhere in the world; if it can't fulfill that promise, the customer gets the part free. That's how sure Cat is, in the first place, that its machines work. Once again, we are looking at a degree of over-achievement that in narrow economic terms would be viewed as a mild form of lunacy; lunacy that is, until you look at Caterpillar's financial results. *Fortune* magazine was quoted as saying that this seemed to be operating on the same principles as Boy Scout law, while *Business Week* wrote that 'product quality was held by Cat people as close as a catechism'.

Motor distributors and the garage trade are a breed the public loves to hate. Most individuals have, at one time or another, had experiences of ostensibly reputable main dealers – not just cowboys – who have tried to sell unnecessary repairs or replacement parts to their customers, or whose work was just unsatisfactory. One big dealer chain, Lex, recognized the problem as applying to some extent to them and, faced with problems of inadequate customer service in the 1980s and the failure of old-fashioned disciplinary action, Lex scrapped the middlemen – the service departments that separated the mechanics from the customers. By bringing customers into direct contact with the mechanics doing the work, they believed they achieved improvements in quality of work, motivation of mechanics and customer confidence.

Some high street banks have come in for a great deal of criticism in the last few years for apparent lack of interest in personal clients, poor personal service and insensitive branch closures. This trend has partly been the result of cost pressures. In contrast, a new, low-cost competitor seized the opportunity, for First Direct aims to be customer-led. The whole operation is based on what the customer wants, namely speed, convenience, service and value for money. It has a small staff, each member of which feels highly valued; it is characterized by good leadership and mutual trust. It gained half a million customers in the first six years of its existence and has proved a formidable competitor to the traditional high-street banks, including its parent within the HSBC Group, Midland.

Keeping customer confidence when things go wrong

Another key aspect of customer service is the way in which complaints are handled. Responsible and rapid action in dealing with complaints is both ethical and obviously good business. Yet the number of companies that prevaricate, delay, send irrelevant standard letters and generally give the idea that the customer is a nuisance, is legion. They demonstrate a total lack of interest in service and start from the premise that the customer is either wrong or trying to pull a fast one. Companies that have properly trained staff to deal with such matters in a professional manner can not only avoid that ultimate sign of failure, the exasperated letter to the MD, but also turn complaints into positive business opportunities.

In even more serious situations, when a company is faced with a problem – whether of its own making or not – where the public is put at risk, crisis management can be a competitive issue. In such a situation the risk may be statistically so small that one company will decide to do nothing in order to save money, while another will be so keen to preserve its reputation that it will go to enormous lengths, sometimes at huge cost, to ensure that the risk is reduced to the absolute minimum. In such instances, the hard decisions are usually governed by the values and ethics of the company.

The best example is in all the textbooks, but it deserves a place here, both for its own sake and because the ethical standards of the company have stood it in good stead in the marketplace. The company is Johnson & Johnson (J&J) and the product was Tylenol. In 1982 an unknown criminal poisoned Tylenol pain relief capsules with cyanide and seven people in the Chicago area died. Johnson & Johnson and its manufacturing affiliate McNeil immediately alerted the public, the media, the medical community and the US Food and Drug Administration. Production of the capsules stopped and they were taken off the shelves at once all over the country. (Tylenol *tablets* were not withdrawn). Only two further bottles of contaminated capsules were found, but no one else died.

The handling of this crisis in the interests of the public and the good name of the company was an admirable exercise of crisis management, greatly helped by the company's *Credo* which had been written in the mid-1940s by Robert Wood Johnson, who headed the company for some fifty years. He was a pioneer of the principles of corporate social responsibility that went far beyond sales and profits. James E Burke, J&J Chairman at the time of the crisis, said: 'We got through Tylenol by drawing on ninety years of public trust in the bank.' Indeed, the publicity J&J got for its responsible approach meant that they recovered market share remarkably quickly: 70 per cent within five months.

In spite of introducing tamper-free packaging for some products, J&J suffered a further incident in 1986 in Winchester County, New York. Its previous experience and the *Credo* again stood it in very good stead. This time all capsules were withdrawn and replaced by 'caplets', and 90 per cent market share was recovered in five months. One columnist, Tom Blackburn of the *Miami News*, wrote: 'J&J is in business to make money. It has done that very well. But when the going gets tough, the corporation gets human, and that makes something special in the bloodless business world.' This is indeed a good example of admirable behaviour (at very considerable cost) proving to be very good for competitiveness in very difficult circumstances. Of course J&J's competitors tried to take advantage of the situation, though not, according to the company, 'by doing anything overt or in bad taste', and they were not very successful.

An example from the UK on a far smaller scale was said to have cost another company £5 million, but did little long-term damage to its share price and may even have improved its image. In 1991 London's Metropolitan olice unearthed an Animal Liberation Front scheme to tamper with Lucozade, the well-known glucose drink made by SmithKline Beecham. As with Tylenol, the company was a victim of an external threat, but it handled the crisis well, withdrawing five million bottles and setting up a consumer 'hotline', thereby ensuring public safety but at the same time achieving a considerable PR success.

The key ethical question is whether a company in such circumstances is prepared to come clean in the real interests of the public and not to try to keep the incident quiet (as some do) in the hope of riding the crisis. When the problem is an internal one, there is even less justification for holding back, however small the statistical risk.

Car manufacturers have over many years provided examples of design problems discovered after launch, which result in dangers to the public of varying seriousness and a threat to their own reputations and profits. Large-scale recalls of vehicles already sold are examples of responsible handling of such problems. For instance, in 1996 there were press reports that Ford had recalled more than eight million cars in the US and Canada for a repair to a faulty ignition switch that could cause overheating in the steering column with a consequent very slight fire risk. The irony for Ford was that only a very small number of the cars concerned would be affected, but to make absolutely certain they were incurring a cost of about $970 million.

In contrast, Perrier handled their own internal problem of bottled water contamination so badly that the Food and Drug Administration forced them to withdraw the product in the US. They lost both market share and their independence as a company.

Customers are more likely to buy from companies that are seen to be ethical

It is quite useless for a highly moral company to expect people to buy from it if its products are uncompetitive. Ethics are no substitute for business excellence, but they are an admirable clincher for competitiveness when a company's product is largely comparable with that of its rivals. As the Johnson & Johnson case above shows, it had the ideal combination of a first-class product and a clear ethical stance on which to draw. Indeed, the best situation is when a company succeeds in matching its corporate values to those of customers and is alert to future trends.

The most obvious example of such a company is the Body Shop, which has done more than any other to emphasize its commitment to environmentally friendly products and responsible policies relating to purchasing from third-world countries. It seeks through its point-of-sale material to ally itself with its customers' own views on these matters.

One of the most important aspects of the trust earned by companies in retailing relates to price, which is appreciated most of all by people who have not got the time to 'shop around'. The John Lewis Partnership's slogan 'Never knowingly undersold' and the way it honours it sets the standard for others. The price wars between the grocery chains led them to offer twice the difference if they were undersold. The petrol companies' desperate measures to halt the gains in market share by the supermarkets led them to adopt 'price watch' schemes. Even in these situations, the consumer still prefers to buy from the company they trust, rather than from one offering the lowest possible price.

That trust will depend on other factors. For example, Marks & Spencer set the scene by taking back unwanted or incorrectly selected goods without quibble long before the law established consumers' rights in the matter in certain circumstances. The goodwill that it created in those early days has stood it in good stead ever since.

In the last analysis there is no question that the best service to customers can be expected from those companies that understand the need to employ people who are properly trained and motivated and are therefore loyal to their employers. That loyalty is achieved by treating them right and enabling them to share in the company's ideals.

TREATING EMPLOYEES AS THE MOST VALUABLE ASSET

To say that people matter more than any other business asset seems trite in the extreme, yet the way in which people have been shed in large numbers in the last years of this century and the way many of them have been treated make one wonder whether it is. Cynics used to say that the role of personnel departments in large companies was to turn people into personnel. The question is whether changing the words really reflects any improvement. The modern expression 'human resources' has an unpleasant and impersonal ring to it, unless of course it is truly understood to mean putting people above physical resources.

The undeniable fact is that the shift in developed countries from manufacturing into service industries and retailing has brought with it a notable reduction in the weight of plant and fixed assets on balance sheets and a corresponding increase in the importance of people, who do not appear on them at all.

However, there are many manufacturing companies that do acknowledge in writing how important their employees are. Ford is a good example: 'Our people are the source of our strength. They provide our corporate intelligence and determine our reputation and vitality. Involvement and teamwork are our core human values.' People are also given prominence in BOC's statement of *Vision and Values*, stressing communication, listening, telling employees how they are getting on through appraisal, individual development and training and succession planning. Similarly, Shell says 'it is recognised that commercial success depends on the full commitment of all employees'.

Retailers need to recognize the importance of people even more, if only because they are dealing directly with the public. Not all of them say it in so many words, but W H Smith is an exception:

> For our staff we should aim to give a good career at whatever level. We must recruit the best people for the job. We must aim to reward people well, train and develop them for their job and for promotion and provide good conditions for work. We must communicate and consult with them, set high standards, always be fair and treat every individual with a sense of dignity. We want to make work enjoyable and rewarding.

The revival of another retailer, Asda, has already been mentioned. One of the key elements was Archie Norman's approach to people. Old-fashioned hierarchical management structures and the symbols that went with them were eliminated. Job titles were changed to refer to the job rather than the rank, while people, whatever their job, found themselves referred to, and treated, as colleagues. 'We want,' said Norman to Lynda King Taylor, 'to be an employer of first choice.'

General statements of this kind need to be borne out in practice. One way of course is to encourage share ownership or, as in the case of the John Lewis Partnership, to make all employees partners in the company. Stuart Hampson, the John Lewis Chairman, in the speech which has already been quoted in Chapter 5, underlined the direct link between treating people right and customer service in the following words: '... if you want to satisfy the customer, you start by putting the employee first.'

Sometimes quite small gestures can be made which show due respect for employees. Monthly-paid employees are generally paid at the end of the month, when they have fulfilled their contract. Some employers take the view that it is fairer to pay their staff in the middle of the month, thus splitting the difference with them – two weeks paid in arrears and two in advance. There is an added advantage that no special pay arrangements need to be made at Christmas, while it is helpful to some employees in the summer holiday period as well. This practice may affect company cash flow and be unpopular with finance directors, but is greatly appreciated by employees.

Earlier in this chapter there was mention of the increased emphasis by larger companies on respecting 'human rights' where traditionally this was seen largely as applying to employees. In this case perhaps a better expression is respect for human dignity and the development of people. What does this mean? In the negative sense it means of course avoidance of discrimination on grounds of colour, race, religion, gender and, it must be added, of age. On the positive side it means a commitment to promote capabilities through career development and access to adequate education and training.

All priceless assets need to be kept in good shape. When those assets are people, this means that training has to have a high priority. No company would disagree that it is in its own interest to make sure it has a qualified workforce with the necessary skills to perform to the best advantage. The idea of including in such training the inculcation of company values to ensure the highest possible ethical performance has a far lower level of support. Training people so that they will be able to get better jobs if they are made redundant would seem excessively altruistic to many business leaders, even though this is ethically desirable in the modern world.

Unfortunately, training, in spite of lip service often paid to it, is one of the easiest costs to cut when times are tough. And too many UK companies did just that during the last two recessions. An exception to this generalization came from the travel industry during the Gulf War. Because of the war, the long-haul operators suffered a downturn, especially of course to Middle Eastern destinations. The reaction of some travel operators was to make staff redundant but Kuoni, one of the market leaders, took the view that this provided a good opportunity to increase staff training.

All these points were recognized when Investors in People (details in Appendix G) was set up in the UK to establish standards to which employers would sign up and demonstrate their commitment to the training and development of their employees. The RSA *Tomorrow's Company* report summed up the importance of training in the context of this book quite simply when it said: 'Education and training are therefore being seen less as issues of cost, and more as preconditions for competitive success.'

Companies, if they are to compete effectively, need employees who are loyal, who are motivated to do their jobs more than just adequately, and who care about how customers are served. Above all, they need people whose personal principles are supported and not jeopardized by the way the company competes.

As for employees:

> Most... are looking for more than just a job. They are looking to identify with the value of their work. They want to feel pride in what they do, to feel that they are working for a company they admire and respect, to sense that their contribution is both real and recognized... Creating shareholder value might be motivational for some senior executives, but isn't going to make the majority of workers in a company leap out of bed in the morning. People look for a company's values, for its soul and then they can begin to believe in it.

This was how Stuart Hampson, the John Lewis Chairman, put it in a speech to the RSA's Forum for Ethics in the Workplace in 1998. He had been a member of the team that produced the RSA's *Tomorrow's Company* Report and made it clear that he regarded loyalty and commitment to be reciprocal. By this he meant that senior management must themselves have a commitment to the company and 'cannot simply be mercenaries. Leadership is long term... directors (and more specifically chief executives) undertake a commitment. In my book, whatever the contract says, a chief executive cannot simply walk out because a better offer comes along.' These somewhat unfashionable words are in contrast to the way some employees are exploited and the way many business leaders exhibit more concern for self-enrichment than leadership, as described in Chapter 5.

Hampson was quite clear that this is indeed a competitive issue: 'I am firmly convinced that companies [that] do not fully respect their relationship with their employees are missing out on a powerful driver to business advantage.' His own company's performance over ten years, as set out in Appendix D, lends powerful support to this line of argument.

ATTRACTING INVESTORS

In the last analysis, the most important of all the stakeholders to the overwhelming majority of businesses is the investor. Without investors risking corporate or personal capital, no business can survive and so bring benefits to the other stakeholders. While business people take this seemingly obvious statement for granted, they still need to be ready to explain it to people who might otherwise support the general argument of this book but still believe, unfortunately, that profit is a dirty word. Profit is essential both for reinvesting in the business and for providing a return to investors. This principle is supported by the law, being enshrined in the articles of association, while in practice investors compete with one another to achieve the best returns in the form of dividends or capital value.

Conversely, companies compete all the time with one another for investment support, whether it be from shareholders, or from banks in the form of borrowings. In the context of this book, the best companies are those that can convince investors to take a long-term view of the benefits arising from their positive ethical attitudes and actions as described in this chapter. If it is true that investors, especially in the City of London, really have a heavy responsibility for seeking short-term profits at the expense of long-term returns, then it is essential for such companies to redress the balance. This was a particular recommendation of the RSA's *Tomorrow's Company* report: '... company leaders will be able to participate in more [open dialogue] with the investment community. They will be able to enlist the help of investors, and those who advise them, in concentrating their minds not only on immediate performance, but also on longer-term prospects.'

In addition to convincing investors of the quality and integrity of their management, companies need to display that they are both ethical and prudent in the face of the law. Compliance with the law, not least on environmental matters where fines can now be very substantial, is of course a basic competitive requirement from the point of view of investors. Some of the large insurance companies are not only taking this view as investors, but also as underwriters. Such investment decisions are often taken because responsibility over environmental matters is usually a sign that the company is managed better in other ways as well.

The UK's Goode Report on Pensions Law Reform distinguishes between these positive reasons for seeking to invest in the sort of companies described in this chapter and the negative reasons for avoiding investment in others. This raises an interesting question, namely whether it is more ethical for investors to support companies for positive ethical reasons or to withhold investment on negative grounds.

The growth of 'ethical' investment funds of various kinds in recent years is evidence that subjective ethical considerations are now gaining ground alongside traditional, objective, hard-nosed financial criteria. 'Ethical' funds are either unit or investment trusts designed for private investors or the capital of pension funds, local authorities, charities or churches, whose investment decisions are swayed by ethical considerations. Some investors are prepared on ethical grounds to accept a less favourable return than might be obtained elsewhere.

The argument deployed by these organizations is that 'ethical' investment can make a difference, by informing companies in a language they understand that unacceptable products and practices will not attract the vital finance they need. Richard Harries, Bishop of Oxford, adopted a high profile on this matter in relation to the investments of the Church of England Commissioners. In his book *Is There a Gospel for the Rich?*, he wrote that the modern ideas on ethical investment that put principles before returns stem from the condemnation of usury by the medieval Church. Recognizing that today money is power, he argued that Christians could help bring about moral improvements through their investments. This can lead to a seeming paradox, namely that investors such as the Church Commissioners might be encouraged to invest in industries of which they disapprove – not just buying one share, as some pressure groups and private individuals do, in order to make a stir at AGMs – but in order to try to wield real influence.

The main companies that are avoided for negative reasons are those concerned with products or services that some people consider to be unacceptable, such as armaments, alcohol, tobacco and gambling, those with poor employment practices or those that operate in countries with unacceptable régimes. Judgments on questions of this kind are often based on prejudice, while the real ethical considerations are inevitably as varied as they are subjective. The case of the pressure on Western companies to pull out of South Africa under apartheid and the experience of Shell in Nigeria have already been mentioned in the previous chapter.

As regards products, there are obvious problems where investors may approve of nearly all that a company does, but object to only one product line (maybe insignificant as a contributor to profits), so precluding them from investing in the rest. Alternatively, one investor can favour a company making products that are of real benefit to the environment, while another can exclude that same company because it is involved in a country with a regime of which he or she disapproves. This means that in practice 'ethical' funds may find themselves excluded from investing in most of the largest companies, because some activity somewhere fails to meet the criteria laid down. For example, one such fund, Friends Provident Stewardship, was only able in mid-1997 to invest in fifteen of the one hundred largest UK companies.

Investment trusts representing thousands of small shareholders and pension funds representing hundreds of thousands of pensioners are faced with a very real problem in this respect. Clearly the fiduciary and ethical duty of those responsible for the funds' management is to achieve the best possible results for their investors and members, whose disparate views on ethical questions cannot possibly be reflected in investment decisions. Needless to say, there is plenty of selective quoting of statistics on both sides of the argument as to whether ethical funds are *per se* a good investment, but naturally many investors are prepared to sacrifice some profits if they feel principles are involved. In the early 1960s the Chairman of Distillers, the manufacturers of the harmful drug Thalidomide, which has already been mentioned in Chapter 5, received a number of letters from shareholders saying they would gladly accept a reduction in dividends if swift action could be taken to compensate the victims.

There can also be conflict between the supposed interests of people when they are working and after their retirement. The view of Arthur Scargill, as President of the National Union of Mineworkers, was that the mineworkers' pension scheme should not invest, *inter alia*, in oil companies, as they were competing with the coal industry. In the court case that followed, *Cowan v Scargill*, the ruling was that the best interests of the pensioners were financial and that ulterior reasons should not override them, a point that Arthur Scargill strongly opposed. In such a situation, both sides can claim the ethical high ground, or can be shown to be moved by practical considerations only, but it goes to show that there are no easy answers as to what is 'right'.

Furthermore, situations can change, facing investors with hard choices. For example, socially responsible companies, which are well thought of by the 'ethical' investment community, can easily lose approval when times are tough, because cutting social expenditure is much easier than, for instance, making people redundant. On ethical grounds, which is the better course anyway? The choice is not easy to make.

There are no simple answers as to whether 'ethical' investment is, in principle, right. Indeed there are people who question whether it *is* ethical, just because it is so hard to decide objectively which companies deserve such support and which do not. This may be one of the reasons why, while there is increasing interest in such investment and funds are growing fast, they still represent only a tiny proportion of the total. According to The Ethical Investment Research Service (EIRIS), funds managed by ethical unit and investment trusts had grown to £1.47 billion by June 1997. As some £150 billion was the total sum under management in unit and investment trusts in the UK that year, penetration was still only about one per cent of the total. This is not, of course, the whole story, because ethical considerations may influence other investors from time to time in ways that cannot be quantified, but it does get the position of 'ethical' investment into some perspective.

However, more ground seems to have been made in the US. According to Rushworth M Kidder, President of the Institute of Global Ethics, based in Camden, Maine, ethical investment in the US in 1997 accounted for $650 million, or ten per cent of the nation's invested funds – a more significant proportion.

A survey by Crédit Suisse in the UK in 1997 showed that more than nine out of ten independent financial advisers (IFAs) believe that companies must commit themselves to ethical policies if they are to succeed, and that irresponsible companies would fail. The survey also showed that the majority of individual clients with ethical views were women and young professionals aged 25 to 40. Not unexpectedly, most IFAs contrasted these individual views with the pension funds that were rarely interested in ethical investment.

'Ethical' investment is not a passing phase, but it could make a much greater difference if 'ethical' investors were to support companies with a positive ethical approach to competition, rather than merely refusing to invest in those whose activities – or some of them – incur their subjective, and sometimes ill-informed, disapproval.

Rightly or wrongly, one of the demands arising from the 'ethical' investment movement is for more ethical and social 'auditing' and more information on the results. This topic is dealt with in the section that follows.

ETHICAL AUDITING AND REPORTING

It has been said that companies should be *accountable* to shareholders and *responsible*, not only to them, but to other stakeholders. This view is shared by many business people today. However, there is a growing climate of opinion that the extent of the influence and power of larger companies is making it more and more necessary to become accountable beyond the shareholder circle.

As pointed out in the preceding section, accountability to shareholders includes conformity with laws and regulations, thus avoiding financial penalties and damage to reputation. This is of course a key competitive requirement. Herein lies a problem: reputation depends not merely on matters of fact such as good products and conformity with the law, but on the highly subjective perceptions of the public.

One of Shell's difficulties over the disposal of the Brent Spa oil platform was that, as a highly responsible company with a *Statement of General Business Principles* that was first brought out in 1976, it rigorously examined the technical pros and cons of different options and made absolutely sure that the preferred solution conformed with all relevant rules and regulations and thus had government approval. What took Shell by surprise was the significance of perceptions about its proposed action and the emotions and prejudices of a relatively small section of the public, especially in Germany, which were whipped up by campaigners, some of whose information was subsequently shown to be inaccurate. All this was compounded by sections of the media so that, as one Shell employee said wryly, 'complex technical issues were turned into soundbites'. This in turn led to very serious acts of violence against Shell installations and threats to individual employees. Although cost had little to do with the argument, it would have been easier for Shell had this solution been more expensive than some of the alternatives. Maybe a less reputable company might have made sure that the preferred option for disposal was not the cheapest!

Here was a company of particularly high standards, whose employees were genuinely personally hurt (and in some cases scared for the safety of their families) to find how strong the hostile perceptions of them were. They learned that nowadays there is a need for a form of accountability that exceeds traditional concepts of responsibility and which requires expertise that goes far beyond traditional public relations skills.

One of the best-known quotations from a speech at the second World Industry Conference on Environmental Management (WICEM II) at Rotterdam in 1991 was from the chemical industry, public perceptions of which are even more negative than those of oil companies. Dave Buzzelli of Dow said: 'Don't trust us, track us. Watch us as we dedicate ourselves to performance improvement.' He recognized that the less business is trusted the more communication, transparency and prior dialogue there has to be. Unwelcome as all this is to hard-pressed traditional directors and managers, more and more time has to be spent on listening to critics.

Up to the 1980s, most companies preferred to have little or nothing to do with NGOs or representatives of the media, who were themselves seen to be in business to be critical of them. Companies preferred to keep their heads below the parapet; even on occasions when they felt forced out into the open over accusations that appeared to be either plain wrong or at least exaggerated, they too often appeared defensive. Some of their top people, preferring recorded television interviews to live appearances, found themselves subjected to brutal and unethical editing, which put their remarks out of context and in the worst possible light.

This changed in the decade that followed, with more business representatives being better prepared and more willing to take the risk of participating in debates and ensuring their point of view did not go by default. Moreover, there is much more dialogue with NGOs, especially the environmental pressure groups, the most constructive being those taking place out of the public eye, where the companies are actually asking the NGOs for advice and the latter are learning how to temper some of their more impractical ideals with sensible realities.

Greater openness and willingness to engage in dialogue on ethical matters has inevitably led to greater pressures on companies to audit performance against the standards they set themselves and to report on them. The first ideas on adding some sort of social audit to annual reports are often ascribed to George Goyder, whose books have already been mentioned earlier in this chapter. Interest in the subject spread more widely in the early 1970s, but the oil crises and economic problems of that decade and later tended to put them on the back burner.

It was in the 1970s that some companies began to refer to their environmental performance in their annual reports, and by the 1990s the practice of conducting internal environmental audits and publishing specific reports on performance in that field became firmly established. The quality of such reports began to become in themselves a competitive issue, with the establishment of annual prizes, such as that offered by the Association of Chartered and Certified Accountants (ACCA). Most companies regarded their reports as first and foremost aimed at informing their own employees, and thereby encouraging them to commit themselves to environmental improvement, but a growing interest was shown in them, not only by environmental campaigners, but also by other stakeholders.

Environmental reporting was the first major departure from traditional, statutory, financial reporting, and it created a precedent for applying similar principles to the wider question of ethical performance and social responsibility. This could in due course become accepted as a competitive issue if the general argument of this chapter were more widely agreed and the ethical investment movement gained further ground. The purpose of such reports would be to:

- inform stakeholders on ethical questions not covered in financial statements;

- demonstrate acceptance of the principle that there is a degree of accountability to society as well as to shareholders;

- examine performance against companies' own codes and in comparison with competitors.

The method advocated by those who are most in favour of this development is a social audit, conducted regularly, systematically and comprehensively and then reported upon with external validation, as is now widely accepted for environmental reports. This issue arose at the Shell AGM in London in May 1997. In a concerted effort, various institutions, among which churches were conspicuous, supported by critical NGOs, proposed a Resolution that internal and external audits be carried out on Shell's 'environmental and corporate responsibility policies, including those policies relating to human rights' (this last referring to Nigeria, as explained earlier in this chapter), and that there should be regular reports to shareholders on the implementation of such policies.

The Board strongly opposed this Resolution, saying that, although they shared the objectives set out in it, they rejected its specific proposals on a point of principle and on technical grounds. In essence, the Resolution appeared to demand a say in the auditing of the Company's *policies* (which the Board could not accept) as well as of how those policies were implemented (which it did accept). In other words, the Shell had had such policies and standards in place for many years and the responsibility for them was theirs alone. This was a clear statement of the company's duty to manage itself in the best interests of shareholders. A skilful publicity campaign was mounted by the sponsors of the Resolution to persuade other institutional and private shareholders to vote in favour of it. Normally such a move would have been lucky to win one per cent of the votes, but this time they gained the support of eleven per cent – still a clear victory for the Board but a warning for the future.

The whole affair was described by one journalist as a 'public relations disaster', but in fact the company had moved a long way since Brent Spa. The 21-year-old *Statement of General Business Principles*, which had already been modified to include reference to human rights for the first time, was described by one commentator as one of the most striking statements of principles in the world (see Appendix F). In 1997 Royal Dutch/Shell produced its first group-wide Health, Safety and Environment (HSE) Report, while Shell UK and the main core businesses produced externally verified HSE reports of their own. In effect, therefore, external verification has been accepted and the process can be expected to continue.

Shell was already seen to be understanding, as never before, the need to be much more sensitive to external perceptions, not least when they are based on incorrect or incomplete information or just plain wrong. It now recognizes the need for more robust and transparent mechanisms to explain its activities to the outside world because, in its own words, 'any gap, whether perceived or real, between policy and performance poses not only a threat to business operations but also a reputational risk'.

Shell and other companies saw long ago that there are considerable risks in all this. Firstly, reports of the kind being demanded are bound to contain material that is both highly subjective and very difficult to quantify, thus making comparisons difficult. Secondly, the demand for yet another type of company report begs the question of whether the cost of preparation and distribution can really be justified and whether the implied transparency will not in fact be obscured by 'information fatigue' – mountains of extra paper read by few apart from the campaigners who demand it.

Yet some business leaders already accept that, as companies have to be seen to be more open, so they must widen the scope of what they report. Some while before Shell's experience with Brent Spa, Lord Alexander, Chairman of NatWest Bank (already quoted earlier), wrote: 'We must not resent the ever-increasing number of reports we have to publish – they are vital if we are to win and keep the confidence of all our stakeholders.' Companies need to heed Lord Alexander's advice, not least because audits will otherwise be conducted by hostile outsiders, as has happened already, especially on environmental questions. Such confrontational activities can be highly damaging, especially when, as Shell has seen only too clearly, the objectivity of the critics is clouded by their prejudices.

It does look, therefore, as though the 'social audit' and subsequent reporting is here to stay and that the way such audits are conducted will evolve with experience. It will also breed a new type of consultant whose main selling point in offering services to companies will be an ability to apply some degree of objectivity to measurements which, by their very nature, are bound to be both imprecise and subjective. One such specialist is Kirk Hanson of Stanford University, who was retained by the Body Shop to undertake a pioneering *Social Evaluation*, published in 1996. Hanson made no bones about the task being far from simple. He wrote in that study:

> Practical problems abound in performing a social or stakeholder audit. What are the dimensions of social performance, for example? Everything a company does affects a stakeholder, you might argue, but you cannot report effectively on everything... What is a social rating? Do you rate a company on some absolute quantitative scale, against some measure of "best practice", against the average behaviour of comparable companies, perhaps against the company's own goals or its claims about its own behaviour?

Because of its self-imposed position on the moral high ground (which Graham Searjeant in *The Times* described as wearing 'its founders' values too boldly on its sleeve' for his taste), the Body Shop ran a considerable risk that the media would give more attention to the negative criticisms than to Hanson's conclusion that on most social matters the company is more responsible and performs above average, even though it was given a low rating on its 'prickly and defensive reaction to criticism'.

Writing of the matter in general terms, Hanson wrote: 'I believe the social audit will eventually be done much as the financial audit is now done – by insiders with outside attestation so that the results present a fair representation of the social performance of the company.' Even recognizing his obvious vested interest in making this statement, Hanson may well be right. As far as companies' ethical performance is concerned, there can be no doubt that, as more and more of them develop codes, the more demand there will be for them to report on their performance against those codes and that this will itself increasingly become a competitive issue.

CONCLUSION

This chapter has tried to show that ethics are good for business, and indeed a key element of competitiveness, just as good business is a truly ethical activity. No one can deny that business exercises great power in society – power to do harm or to do good. Some people exaggerate the extent of that power, but whatever those views may be, all agree that business has to exercise responsibility commensurate with it. This demands a high degree of harmony with all stakeholders and, if this is recognized in their perceptions of the company, it is indeed an important aspect of competitiveness.

The idea that ethical behaviour is an element of competitiveness has led to cynical questions as to whether it is indeed ethical to compete on ethics. Doing so can only be effective when it is seen to be truly genuine and embedded in the values and ethos of the company, and not just a glossy creation of public relations departments.

It is to be hoped that readers will agree that the case has already been made. The final short chapter will try to draw together the arguments in favour of competition itself as an essentially ethical idea and the proposition that competing in an ethical manner *is* good for business.

Chapter 8

Summing up

The market is not a perfect instrument. The 'invisible hand' gets very shaky at times. Competition too can be imperfect and can make life very difficult for people in business, especially because it seems to get tougher all the time through new technologies, the information revolution, and the emergence of new competitors from all over the world. As a rule, the stronger competition is, the more beneficial it is to the consumer. This is the essence of its validity from both the utilitarian and the ethical point of view. On the other hand, it also increases the challenges to business and so raises the temptation to cut moral corners.

Companies and the individuals who work in them need to recognize that, in competing with all the strength and skill that they can deploy, there are rules that reach out well beyond those actions that can or should be within the scope of the law. They should certainly strive to be winners, but not at any cost. As has happened time and time again, disregard for those principles brings competition in particular and business in general into disrepute, only confirming the doubts and prejudices of the critics.

Concerned about these prejudices, Tim Melville-Ross said in a speech in June 1997:

> The business community as a whole, working through many different agencies, must launch a movement which makes a concerted effort to:
>
> - improve public understanding of business;
> - change the poor perception of the values and behaviour of business people;
> - change the behaviour of some business people which reinforces this perception.

In the context of this book, the three points need to be addressed simultaneously, although the third is an essential prerequisite to the other two. The movement is already there, with many organizations (some of which are listed in Appendix G) working in their different ways to help raise standards in business, especially when competition might make them want to cut corners. This book is intended to be a modest contribution to that movement.

In *Thought for the Day* in May 1996, part of which has already been quoted, Charles Handy said:

> Sometimes I think that if the British really do have a disdain for business, it is not because they despise the idea of making money, but because they distrust the ethical soundness, the sense of fairness, of some of the people who make the money. A good business is not just profitable, it is also just, giving each their due. That matters more now than ever before, because almost everything today seems to be a business of a sort – schools, hospitals, agencies, you name it. We are customers now, wherever we go. That's great, in a way – competition does sort the sheep from the goats in terms of efficiency – but efficiency for what end, and for whom? We have to trust their leaders to get the balance right and we must just hope that their ethics are as good as their sums.

It has been the intention of this book to make the case for including ethical standards in the competitive process – to help readers make sure the ethics *are* as good as the sums. There are plenty of people in business who feel that ethics are somehow a luxury to be enjoyed when times are good, something to which successful business people can pay lip service to towards the end of their careers. Ethics to some people are a form of excess baggage that has to be shed when the company is forced to slim down in order to face up to tough competitors who are not so encumbered. In such situations it is not easy for individuals to stand on matters of principle, thus risking the job security of themselves and colleagues. To them the answer to the question posed by the title of this book: *Competitive and Ethical?* may be 'No, sorry, it's just not realistic.'

Any reader who expected simple, gift-wrapped solutions to the quite extraordinarily difficult and diverse moral problems that business people face day-to-day may feel disappointed. However, there is no need for despair; there is a growing recognition by responsible business enterprises that high ethical standards are important, while there is an increasing amount of moral support and practical advice available from many sources, both inside and outside companies.

The advice is worth heeding, especially for its own sake on moral grounds, but also for practical reasons. Every time enterprises fail to get the ethics right, the regulators are called in, descending on businesses in an avalanche of red tape, which only too often ends up limiting or even destroying the effectiveness of competition.

Ken Rushton, Group Secretary of ICI, said at the launch of a publication of the Institute of Business Ethics in October 1997: 'The whole area of business conduct goes to the heart of a company's reputation... It is plain business common sense to have high ethical standards based on core values.' Talking of trust, he said: 'Without it, business is dead in the water.'

This sums up so well what this book has been trying to say. Companies that are really well managed and achieve the right balance between serving all the stakeholders, as described in the last chapter, are those that are most likely to remain competitive in the long run. For them there is no need to find their values and standards of conduct a hindrance to their competitiveness; on the contrary, they are the essential building blocks for tomorrow's company.

Winston Churchill, in his famous defence of democracy in the House of Commons in 1947, said that it was 'the worst form of government except all those other forms that have been tried from time to time'. The same applies to competition: it may be far from perfect, it can be misused, but it is still far better than any of the alternatives. Because of its imperfections, people of principle must compete hard, but in such a way that it remains worthy of celebration.

In which case, the answer to the question posed by the title of this book is a resounding 'yes'. You can indeed be competitive *and* ethical.

References

The deliberate absence of footnotes in the text means that the precise location of ideas and quotations in the text may be hard to find, but these are some of the books, essays, lectures, etc that have been most helpful in writing this book. Inclusion is in no way an indication of approval, any more than exclusion is a sign of disapproval!

Acton, H B (1993) 'The Ethics of Competition' in *The Morals of Markets and other Essays*, eds D Gordon and J Shearmur, Liberty Press

Beauchamp, T L (1977, revised 1983) *Ethical Theory and Business*, Prentice Hall

Berry, R J (ed.) (1993) *Environmental Dilemmas, Ethics and Decisions*, Chapman & Hall, London; also includes a chapter on Industry by Giles Wyburd

Brigley, Stephen (1994) *Walking the Tightrope*, Institute of Management, London

Brittan, Samuel (1995) *Capitalism with a Human Face*, Edward Elgar

Burke,Tom and Hill, Julie (1990) *Ethics, Environment and the Company*, Institute of Business Ethics, London

Cairncross, Frances (1991) *Costing the Earth,* The Economist Books, London

Fletcher, Joseph (1963) *William Temple, Twentieth Century Christian*, Seabury Press, New York

Friedman, Milton (1972) *Capitalism and Freedom*, The University of Chicago Press

Goyder, George (1961) *The Responsible Company*, Basil Blackwell, Oxford

Goyder, Mark and others (1995) *Tomorrow's Company*, Royal Society of Arts, London

Green, Stephen (1996) *Serving God? Serving Mammon?*, Marshall Pickering

Griffiths, Brian (1984) *The Creation of Wealth,* Hodder and Stoughton, London

Handy, Charles (1994) *The Empty Raincoat: Making Sense of the Future*, Hutchinson, London

Handy, Charles (1997) *The Hungry Spirit*, Hutchinson, London

Harries, Richard (1992) *Is There a Gospel for the Rich?*, Mowbray

Harvey-Jones, John (1988) *Making it Happen*, Collins, London

Hill, Julie (1992) *Towards Good Environmental Practice*, Institute of Business Ethics, London

Hill, Julie and others (1994) *Benefiting Business and the Environment*, Institute of Business Ethics, London

Hutton, Will (1995)*The State We're In*, Jonathan Cape, London; (1996) Vintage, London

Manne, Henry G (1975) 'Corporate Altruism and Individualistic Methodology', a lecture published in *Capitalism and Freedom, Problems and Prospects*, ed. Richard Selden, University Press of Virginia

Moody-Stuart, George (1997) *Grand Corruption*, WorldView Publishing, Oxford

Murray, David (1997) *Ethics in Organisations*, Kogan Page, London

Novak, Michael (1996) *Business as a Calling*, The Free Press

Peters,Thomas J and Waterman, Robert H Jr (1982) *In Search of Excellence*, Harper & Row, New York

Russell, Bertrand (1946), *A History of Western Philosophy*, Allen & Unwin, London

Sacks, Jonathan (1995), *Faith in the Future*, Darton, Longman & Todd, London

Samuelson, Paul A (1964) *Economics: An Introductory Analysis,* 6th Edition, McGraw Hill

Schmidheiny, Stephan (1992) *Changing Course*, MIT, Cambridge, MA, US

Schumacher, E F (1973) *Small is Beautiful,* (1974) Abacus Edition by Sphere Books, London

Sternberg, Elaine (1994) *Just Business: Business Ethics in Action*, Little, Brown, London

Tawney, R H (1926) *Religion and the Rise of Capitalism*; (1938) Pelican Books, West Drayton, Middx.

Taylor, Lynda King (1996) *Corporate Excellence in the Year 2000*, Random House, London

Temple, William (1910) *Principles of Social Progress*, Australian Student Christian Union, Melbourne

Webley, Simon (1992) *Business Ethics and Company Codes*, Institute of Business Ethics, London

Webley, Simon (1993) *Codes of Business Ethics*, Institute of Business Ethics, London

Webley, Simon (1995) *Applying Codes of Business Ethics*, Institute of Business Ethics, London

Webley, Simon (1997) *Codes of Ethics and International Business,* Institute of Business Ethics, London

Wyburd, Giles (1994) *Institutionalising the Fight against Grand Corruption*, seminar report, Worldaware, London

Wyburd, Giles (1996) *The Fight against International Corruption: What the European Union Can Do*, seminar report, Worldaware, London

General reference titles

Business Charter for Sustainable Development, International Chamber of Commerce, Paris

Employees' Health and Organisational Practice, Institute of Business Ethics, London

Extortion and Bribery in Business Transactions (1977, revised 1996), International Chamber of Commerce, Paris

International Codes of Marketing and Advertising Practice (1996), International Chamber of Commerce, Paris

Management and the Health of Employees (1991), Institute of Business Ethics, London

Our Common Future (1987) (otherwise known as the *Brundtland Report*) Oxford University Press, Oxford and New York

Responsibility of the British Public Company, otherwise known as the *Watkinson Report* (1973), Confederation of British Industry, London

The British Codes of Advertising and Sales Promotion (1995), The Committee of Advertising Practice, London

Appendix A

Competition and religion

The three monotheistic religions, Christianity, Judaism and Islam, have each given their overt moral support to the Institute of Business Ethics. Below is an outline of what each has to say about competition and, indeed, to what extent they are or are not in favour of it, or can be said to be neutral on the subject. There is naturally a great deal of common ground between them because of their shared origins.

Common to all three religions is that their basic teaching originated in societies in completely different stages of economic development from ours today. The economic systems of those days were based on agriculture and craft-based manufacturing processes and there was national and international trade, but perhaps too much can be made of an excessively literal transposition of that teaching – which is primarily spiritual – to the economic realities of modern competition. However, because the moral imperatives of the teaching of all three religions are immutable to their followers, they are much more relevant to the way competition is *conducted* than to competition itself and the economic benefits it provides.

THE CHRISTIAN VIEW

'The Christian Church has never found it easy to come to terms with the market place.' So Brian Griffiths (now Lord Griffiths) opened his book *The Creation of Wealth*, which, as a well-known defender of market economics, he wrote in 1984 at the request of the Christian Association of Business Executives, the body which founded the Institute of Business Ethics two years later.

Interpretations from the New Testament

There are many strands of teaching arising out of the Gospels in relation to competition, ranging from the outright hostile to the lukewarm and, as Brian Griffiths has said, 'If we take the Gospels seriously, it seems at first sight as if there is a grave inconsistency between the teachings of Jesus on the subject of wealth and poverty and the principles on which market economies depend for their success.'

According to Griffths, the general theme of much Christian thought is that 'a system of competitive markets, which allows profits to be the criterion for survival and which encourages freedom of individual choice, results in a competitive, greedy, unequal society which runs totally counter to the teachings of Jesus on these subjects... This places the businessman in an intolerable position because it implies he is either corrupt or naïve.'

Hostility, or at best ambivalence, indeed seems to have characterized the Christian attitude to most of what modern competition is about. There has been greater concern about how wealth is distributed than about how it is created, while the hostility of the Church has been aimed at aspects of the market economy such as private profit, private corporations and usury, rather than at competition as such.

Such attitudes reflected the view that competition is only too often associated with the worship of mammon, materialism, immoral activities, exploitation and the fact that people get hurt. These and many of the moral questions discussed in Chapter 1 have all contributed to Christian concerns.

Perhaps even more important are severe reservations about self-interest, which Adam Smith and later the free market economists insisted should be the driving force of competition, yet such Christian reservations can conflict with the equally Christian belief in the human need for challenge, discipline and constant striving for improvement which, in practice, competition stimulates.

The problem seems to be that aggressiveness, which most people would regard as necessary if competition is to be effective, is hardly compatible with the doctrine from the Sermon on the Mount: 'Blessed are the meek.' While recognizing the very real economic benefits, there have always been reservations about whether efficiency fosters the true objectives of life, such as joy, peace and brotherhood.

These views were put forward by William Temple, Archbishop of Canterbury earlier in the twentieth century, whose pronouncements on economics and business had not made him popular with the members of the (then) Federation of British Industry. They objected especially to his early preference for state ownership, a view he later modified due to his distrust of bureaucracy. In his *Principles of Social Progress* Archbishop Temple wrote: 'Competition neither can, nor ought, to be eliminated: we should aim at a society co-operative in principle and competitive in detail.' Here we have the point made in Chapter 1–

namely that Christians believe in co-operation, community and caring for others, which appear at first sight to be at odds with the competitive and individualistic ideals of the market economy. In reality, some say that in spite of the tensions between them, it is a fallacy to place them in opposition to one another; excesses of competition destroy co-operation, while excesses of co-operation stifle initiative and ruin competition.

Temple was a friend of R H Tawney, whose *Religion and the Rise of Capitalism* was first published in 1926. Looking through history from the Middle Ages to the present day, Tawney's theme is consistent: 'A philosophy which treated the transactions of commerce and the institutions of society as indifferent to religion would have appeared not merely morally reprehensible, but intellectually absurd.' Business and industry, in succeeding, 'must satisfy criteria which are not purely economic' and the Christian Church has 'as its centre the superiority of moral principles over economic appetites'. In the context of competition, he admired the undoubted commercial achievements of the late seventeenth and eighteenth centuries of which 'England was the daring, if not too scrupulous, pioneer.' Further, he wrote: 'If... economic ambitions are good servants, they are bad masters.' From this the message was clear: compete by all means, but make sure moral principles prevail.

Two twentieth century Papal Encyclicals have mentioned competition. Pope Pius XI, in *Quadragesimo Anno* (1931), wrote: 'Free competition, though justified and right within limits, cannot be an adequate controlling principle in economic affairs.' And later, in the Encyclical *Populorum Progressio* (1967), Pope Paul VI repeated the same point when he lamented many aspects of liberal capitalism, including 'competition as the supreme law of economics'. These pronouncements were far from an outright condemnation of competition, but relate to the need for there to be some limits to the way in which it should operate, particularly internationally, where poorer countries can be adversely affected.

The Roman Catholic Bishop John Jukes, who has done much to affirm wealth creation in recent years, warns of the 'dangers to the human spirit which arise from riches', but says that he can find 'no place in the Gospels where Jesus is shown as castigating competition as such'. Bishop Jukes states that there is no modern specific teaching on competition in the Catholic tradition (other than the pronouncements in the Encyclicals mentioned above), but plenty of course on the moral problems that can arise from commercial activities. While he acknowledges that some interpretations of the gospels have been thoroughly opposed to competition, he insists that the Catholic Church is neutral on it and thus mainly concerned with the motives that drive it and the consequences that flow from it.

Stephen Green, a director of an international banking group in the City of London, writing as an ordained Anglican minister in his book, *Serving God? Serving Mammon?*, says: 'Too often the Christian Church has spoken out against money and markets from the outside,' while he was seeing it from the inside. In his view, 'the Church leaders did not get their hostility directly from anything Jesus said or did', having had 'little to say about commerce as such'.

It needs saying, that neither Jesus nor the New Testament writers condemned or sanctioned either competition or the alternatives – state or private monopolies or planned economies, in which there is no room for competition to operate. This is because He and they accepted the world as they found it, not being concerned about the economics and politics of their time ('render under Caesar...'). Jesus was, however, concerned with the spiritual *effects* of economic activity, especially the corrupting dangers of riches and the plight of the poor. His teaching on the distributional implications of economic activity has been extended by some Christian thinkers into judgments on the nature of modern wealth creation and the role of competition within that process.

While the New Testament can be said to be neutral about competition itself, it is anything but neutral about the way in which it is conducted, which is the central theme of this book. Richard Harries, currently Bishop of Oxford, in *Is There a Gospel for the Rich?*, wrote: 'There is a major role for competition and the entrepreneur. There is no case for saying that markets work best if left alone.' He went on: 'Organised self-interest is not always a pretty sight, particularly when it takes the form of one company trying to do another down.' But he says that competition is still not wrong and approves of a company 'that seeks to be the best, that to which people can feel proud to belong'.

In Bishop Jukes's words: 'Competition is imperfect; it can be abused; it can be conducted in evil ways; its excesses put human dignity at risk; but it is a fact of life and still seems the best system we have. It must remain the servant of man and not be allowed to become the master.'

Lessons from the Old Testament

Is there more support for competition from the Old Testament and from the Judaeo-Christian tradition? Of the Ten Commandments, there are four that seem relevant. Perhaps the one that has caused most controversy recently concerns respect for the Sabbath day, as many Christians are deeply opposed to Sunday trading, which has developed as a direct result of competition.

Three of the prohibitive Commandments deserve comment in this context: 'Thou shalt do no murder,' 'Thou shalt not steal,' and 'Thou shalt not covet.'

On the first of these, it was Bertrand Russell who commented: 'you may undersell a competitor, but you may not murder him'; Samuel Brittan later made the same point: 'Not even the most libertarian of economists would urge the shooting of competitors.' There is no need to say more on this here, as this book is more concerned with actions not covered by the law than those clearly proscribed by it.

Secondly, although most people would agree that stealing is obviously un-lawful as well as immoral, situations can arise in business which fall within the greyer areas, some of which are touched on in Chapters 3 to 5. A witty, but cyni-cal, comment on this comes from Arthur Hugh Clough's poem, *The Latest Decalogue: an Exercise in Spiritual Doubt*, written in 1862. 'Thou shalt not steal; an empty feat/ When it's so lucrative to cheat.' This is only too often true when competition becomes really tough.

Thirdly, the commandment on coveting may be considered rather more rele-vant, because it is normal to covet one's competitor's market share in business. Clough's comment on this was: 'Thou shalt not covet; but tradition/ Approves all forms of competition.' However, there is a danger that the attraction of this witticism in relation to this book gives it more weight than it deserves.

Samuel Brittan, Brian Griffiths and Stephen Green agree that, in their view, it is far from easy to reconcile Adam Smith's economics and Christian teaching by relying on the New Testament, but it is debatable whether the Old Testament makes it easier. This said, at least on the surface it does appear that Jewish teach-ing is rather more explicitly supportive of competition.

JEWISH INSIGHTS

Jewish thinking has always recognized that 'competition released energy and creativity and served the general good', according to the Chief Rabbi, Jonathan Sacks, in his book *Faith in the Future.* Rabbis in general were 'in favour of mar-kets and competition. These lowered prices and increased choice.' But he went on to say that the rabbis 'were fully aware that competitiveness, as such, was not a virtue'. In particular, Judaism preferred an open competitive market as long as it was to the benefit of society as a whole, which normally coincides with the benefit of the consumer.

Judaism condemns the 'perennial temptations of the market – to pursue gain at someone else's expense, to take advantage of ignorance, to treat employees with indifference', which need to be fought against. Dr Sacks points out that 'canons of fair trading had to be established and policed, the onus being on the seller, as 'Jewish law recognises no concept of *caveat emptor.*'

Interestingly, Jewish law also permits protectionist policies in certain in-stances, to safeguard the local economy, particularly where outside traders have unfair advantages through not paying taxes. Nevertheless, Judaism recognizes that even where firms and individuals suffer from fair competition it is not to the benefit of society to restrain it. Some of the practices discussed in Chapter 5 are frowned on by Judaism because they amount to forms of theft: it appears, for ex-ample, that there would not be much difficulty in accepting loss leaders in mer-chandising, whereas predatory pricing designed solely to knock out competitors would not be acceptable.

Dr Meir Tamari, a world expert on Jewish business ethics, explains this last point as one requiring a balance between efficiency and equity. Thus a distinction is made between the destruction of the competitor's livelihood, which is forbidden, and competition, which is to be encouraged, as it may reduce income but does benefit the community. A further issue that Dr Tamari raises is the injustice seen in the uneven exercise of commercial power between large and small firms.

Dr Tamari expresses strong reservations about the argument of the free-market economists, namely that when companies collapse in the face of competition, market forces move capital and labour into alternative activities. Nevertheless, he makes a strong case for competition in saying that the 'communal–national nature of Judaism, in which society is, as it were, an entity possessing economic rights and obligations' is why the Jewish Law supports 'the communal benefits flowing from competition, seeing the welfare of the majority as having precedence over the interest of the relatively few affected competitors'.

THE MUSLIM APPROACH

The Muslim attitude to competition is also supportive. There is a passage in the Koran: 'Race with each other in doing good.' Islamic law also supports competition by condemning monopolistic practices, which are both illegal and immoral. Furthermore, it is very clear that good must come of competition and is precise on what aspects of competition are not to be allowed, including the giving and receiving of bribes (dealt with in detail in Chapter 4), exploiting employees by not paying fair wages or failing to pay them promptly, while misleading customers with false product claims. In the latter context, the principles established in Islamic Law were included in the UK's Trade Descriptions Act 1968 some 1,400 years later.

One aspect of competition that is more generally accepted in modern society but is greatly disapproved of by the Muslim religion is advertising, especially some of its manifestations that build false images. Advertising includes, for example, the creation of artificial or addictive 'needs', and thus of unnecessary consumption, which is exploitation of both people and the environment. Muslims are also well known for their disapproval of conscious or subconscious exploitation of sexual images, especially involving women in advertising and not least when they have no relevance to the product. Dr Badawi, Principal of the Muslim College in London, agrees that the world would be duller without many of the sophisticated advertisements now appearing on our screens, but feels they would be more acceptable if they were broadcast as entertainment without the insidious marketing messages they often convey!

Islamic Law is also very clear in the matter of a proper balance of responsibility to stakeholders (discussed in Chapter 7). For example, a company must be entirely transparent with its shareholders over the allocation of profit and must be very careful to avoid exploiting either them or its employees at the expense of the other.

In short, the Muslim religion favours competition, providing it is achieved justly and there is no deception, no exploitation and no demeaning of people. While it is very precise on matters of principle relevant to this book, Islamic Law recognizes that they can only be applied where there is visible proof; where this is not the case, the state cannot intervene and matters of ethics are left to the conscience of the individual. It is, of course, precisely this aspect of competition that this book is all about.

THE RELIGIOUS CONSENSUS

It is no surprise that there is a great deal of common ground in the attitudes of these three monotheistic religions, as outlined in the preceding sections. This common ground was reflected in *An Interfaith Declaration, A Code of Ethics on International Business for Christians, Muslims and Jews*, work on which was started under the auspices of the Duke of Edinburgh at St George's House, Windsor, and concluded in Amman in 1993. The *Declaration* confirmed strongly the economic benefits of competition and condemned monopolies in the following statement:

> Competition between businesses has generally been shown to be the most effective way to ensure that resources are not wasted, costs are minimised and prices fair. The State has a duty to see that markets operate effectively, competition is maintained and natural monopolies are regulated. Business will not seek to frustrate this.

The *Declaration* lays down four common principles, all of which have already been mentioned in this book and are its theme throughout: that business (and by implication competition) must be governed by justice (fairness), mutual respect (love and consideration), stewardship (trusteeship) and honesty (truthfulness). Other words that might be added to the list are integrity, creativity, service and leadership.

There will be some cynics who think that these fine words and competition just do not mix. The Institute of Business Ethics held a conference in 1988 in which the three faiths came together to consider the theme of *Business and Society*. Interestingly, the word 'competition' was not mentioned once in the record of the conference, but there was plenty of discussion on how to close the gap between 'moral duties, business acumen and a flourishing economy', in the words of a Muslim speaker. The Chairman, Neville Cooper, quoted a hard-pressed executive who said: 'Business is difficult enough without bringing ethics into it.' For such people, bringing religion into the equation merely muddies the waters and reduces the competitive drive. They fail to understand that this view, carried to its logical conclusion, destroys the moral foundation on which competition depends.

Many people in business are of the view that the concerns of religious teachers about competition are irrelevant, because they are more about the weaknesses of human nature and about individuals than about business. They feel that religious concerns about poverty, inequality and injustice cannot be blamed on competition. On the contrary, they say, competition itself helps to meet human needs efficiently, even though it cannot solve the problem of unfair distribution.

There is, however, broad common ground in the idea that society needs competition between businesses to get the maximum benefit and value from them. In providing that value, all religious and moral teaching is quite clear that there must be ethical standards and restraints on how it is done. That is what the practical chapters in this book are all about.

Appendix B

Extracts from FIDIC's Policy Statement on Corruption

This extract is published by permission of FIDIC, PO Box 86, 1000 Lausanne, Switzerland, from which the full version may be obtained.

Corrupt practices can occur at all stages of the procurement process – in the marketing of engineering services; during the design; in preparing tender documents (including specifications); in pre-qualifying tenderers; in evaluating tenders; in supervising the performance of those carrying out the construction; issuing of payment certificates to contractors; making decisions on contractors' claims.

The selection of a Consulting Engineer is a most important task and is the basis for the essential and mutual client-consultant trust. The various selection criteria advocated by FIDIC, to be applied in judging an engineer's suitability to carry out a project, are completely undermined if the selection process is tainted by corruption. The preparation of a short list is an important part of the process and must be carried out openly.

The Consulting Engineer must not offer or accept remuneration of any kind which may be perceived to attempt, or in reality attempt, to influence the selection or compensation procedure or affect the impartial judgment of the Consulting Engineer.

Therefore, FIDIC recommends as follows:

1. To reduce the opportunities for corruption in the process of procurement of engineering and construction services, qualification-based selection procedures and competitive tendering, respectively, should be used.

2. In implementing particular projects, Consulting Engineers should recommend to their clients the most appropriate and objective procurement process or delivery system, consistent with the demands of the project.

3. Funding agencies should be kept fully informed by the Consulting Engineer of the procurement steps as they occur. The Consulting Engineer shall notify funding agencies of any irregularities, in order that cancellation or other remedies may be exercised in accordance with the loan agreement.

4. Consulting Engineers should be aware of local law regarding corruption and should promptly report criminal behaviour to the proper law enforcement authorities.

5. FIDIC member associations should take prompt disciplinary action against any member firms found to have violated the FIDIC Code of Ethics. This could include, among other actions, expulsion and notification of public agencies. Procedures should be established by member associations to assure that the due process of law is afforded in such cases. The procedure for determining whether the expulsion of a member firm is warranted should be conducted confidentially but expeditiously.

6. Member associations and their members (firms and individuals) should internally develop and maintain systems to protect their high ethical standards and codes of conduct. They should co-operate candidly with other organizations which seek to reduce corruption. Member firms should associate themselves only with other member firms who share similar high ethical standards.

7. Member associations should foster and support the enactment of legislation in their own countries which is aimed at curbing and penalizing corrupt practices.

Appendix C

The John Lewis Partnership

The summary below is an edited and updated version of a brochure produced by the company in March 1997 and produced here with its permission.

The John Lewis Partnership is one of the largest retailers in Britain, with 23 department stores. By 1997 there were 115 Waitrose supermarkets compared with 39 in 1970 with a further vigorous development programme in hand.

In all, the business has well over 100 establishments in locations from Aberdeen to the south coast of England, varying in size from units with 20 employees to one with almost 3,000. Net assets employed as at January 1997 were £1,063 million. 'Partners' (ie staff) totalled 41,100 (excluding part-time employees), and together they did £3,161 million of business.

AIMS

The aim of the John Lewis Partnership is not to be the biggest retail group in Britain but to be the best, the happiest and the most efficient. A great deal of energy is expended on examining the Partnership's social and political organization to encourage the involvement of Partners in the running of their business, to add to the democratic elements in its systems and, as far as possible, to ensure its future by strengthening its institutions.

ORIGINS

In 1864 at the age of 28 John Lewis, who had for some years been a buyer of silks and dress materials for Peter Robinson, set himself up in a small shop in

London's Oxford Street. He was a man of high principles and fixed opinions, who carried into his business and his dealings with subordinates the strictness with which he governed himself.

His methods were scrupulously honest. He gave good value on the basis of low profit margins and skilful buying. He believed in the importance of offering his customers a wide assortment of sizes and colours in the goods that he stocked.

His business prospered steadily and came to have a reputation for value and fair dealing.

The shop was entirely his own property. On the twenty-first birthdays of his sons, Spedan and Oswald, he gave to each a quarter share in the business, thus making it a family partnership.

THE PARTNERSHIP PRINCIPLE

In 1914 Spedan Lewis's chance came. That year his father, who some eight years earlier had bought the controlling interest in Peter Jones Ltd (a department store in London's Sloane Square), made it over to him, telling him that he could do whatever he liked with Peter Jones so long as he did not leave the Oxford Street business before five o'clock in the afternoon. Peter Jones was then making a loss, but Spedan Lewis accepted the challenge and promptly told the staff that if and when the business became profitable they would share the profit. He followed this up with a number of innovations designed to improve working conditions, stimulate free speech and encourage a sense of responsibility and pride in performance.

By 1920 the business was making a profit of £20,000 and in that year the first distribution of 'Partnership benefit' was made in promissory notes, representing no less than seven weeks' pay over and above the full ordinary rates. This was a triumph both for the workers at Peter Jones and for their managing director, Spedan Lewis, who saw in it the first fruits of a principle to which he had devoted so much earnest thought and energy, as well as some confirmation of his shopkeeping abilities.

Upon his father's death in 1928 Spedan Lewis found himself sole owner of the Oxford Street business as well as Peter Jones. He was now able to carry his scheme for Partnership much further. In April 1929 he established a Trust for the benefit of the workers in the two businesses. The broad effect of this First Settlement was that he sold to those workers, present and future, all his dividend rights in the two businesses, and left the capital sum due to him as vendor in the hands of the Partnership as a loan. He was advised that the price of around £1 million was no more than that which he could obtain on the open market. The newly-formed Partnership paid no interest on this loan and was able to spread the repayments over more than 25 years.

It was explicit from the earliest days of the Partnership that workers, who were to be co-owners of the business, should have an appropriate share in its policy and direction. The emphasis is on the word 'appropriate'. No modern business can survive for long unless it is sustained by expert knowledge and controlled by a clear central policy. Therefore the aim has been to secure for the joint owners of the business a degree of democratic influence compatible with perceptive and successful management. This is largely met by the principle of management accountability. Industrial democracy does not necessarily mean the election of managers. Neither does the Partnership agree with those of its critics who maintain that there can be no industrial democracy without conflict. Instead it believes that democracy lies in the accountability of the management to the managed, not just as a theory, but as a hard fact of everyday commercial life.

THE PRINCIPLE IN PRACTICE

In practice this means that those Partners who may neither aspire to be a manager, nor possess the abilities to be one, are recognized as individuals with a valid contribution to make to the success of the business. They have a right to question anything they do not understand and to receive frank answers. Managers in the Partnership are to this extent in the position of professional advisers, accountable to all Partners. This system gives management full scope to be strong and effective but provides that it must operate democratically with due regard to the rights and duties of all concerned. These rights and duties are specified in a written Constitution. The Founder, John Spedan Lewis, made two Settlements in Trust. They can be modified only by consent of a court of law. The First Settlement, made in 1929, provides for the division of the profits among all the Partners (unless, rarely, a Partner is excluded because of individual circumstances). The Second, dating from 1950, provides through trustees for the control of the whole group, that is, the election of some directors and the appointment of the chairman.

This constant development of the machinery of participation can be itemized and measured, and one very tangible way members of the Partnership participate is through any annual profits bonus – just one instance of how the rewards of success are shared at all levels of the business. What is less easy to assess is the effect of the co-ownership structure upon the general atmosphere and character of the Partnership as experienced by those who work in it. Perhaps one indication is the extent to which some Partners are prepared to give their own time to organizing leisure outings for their colleagues and the number of them who enjoy the company of fellow workers out of business hours. Another might be that the general trend of criticism and suggestions which come through the councils, committees for communication and letters to company publications is a constructive one and serves to strengthen and expand the real practice of partnership.

The Partnership has grown steadily in numbers, size and profit, and the many recent developments in both department stores and Waitrose underline its ongoing success. The full involvement of employees is a distinguishing feature of how the company works and is at the heart of the way it competes in the tough conditions of the high street.

Speaking at the launch of the Royal Society of Arts inquiry into what goes into making 'Tomorrow's Company', Stuart Hampson, the Chairman, said: 'Our business is about serving customers so well that they want to come back and shop with us again. Is it any surprise that this task is done better by employees who have a direct financial interest in the profit we make?'

THE PRACTICE PAYS OFF FOR THE BENEFIT OF THE PARTNERS

The figures below speak for themselves. The net profit shown is after tax, being the amount available for Partnership bonus and retention in the business for further development. Bonuses have varied from 8 to 24 per cent on 'ranking' pay (that is the actual amount earned rather than the rate at the time the bonus became due) during the period depending on trading conditions. The lower of these figures (the lowest since the Korean War) reflected the recession, while the higher (one of the best ever) was achieved in the earlier boom years.

The John Lewis Partnership: company statistics 1988–97

£m	1988	1989	1990	1991	1992	1993	1994	1995	1996	1997
Turnover	1724.8	1917.7	2046.3	2159.2	2280.4	2357.3	2420	2575.5	2815.7	3160.5
Net profit	93.5	104.8	88.9	78.7	68.8	62.2	76.8	94.2	121.2	171.7
Partnership bonus	46.2	47.4	41.3	33.1	30.2	28.2	34.5	43.1	57	81.7
Retained in the business	47.3	57.4	66.2	42.1	38.6	34	42.3	51.1	64.2	90
Net assets employed	547.5	593.5	662.2	707.6	747.3	781.3	808.5	861.7	952	1062.5
Partnership bonus (%)	24	22	17	12	9	8	10	12	15	20

Source: annual reports

Appendix D

The John Lewis Rules on gifts and hospitality from suppliers

The Partnership, in common with other reputable companies, has strict Rules on how to conduct its business. Under the heading of Suppliers, there are four Articles (25–28) on the subject dealt with in Chapter 4. They can be summarized as follows:

- there is a prohibition on receiving gifts or rewards from suppliers;

- gifts may be accepted if refusal would cause offence, especially in a foreign country;

- if a gift or hospitality has monetary value, the equivalent should be paid into a fund of the Partnership's, or reciprocated at the Partnership's or the receiver's own expense;

- such offers must be reported to superiors.

This is the actual wording:

Gifts to Partners or private purchases by them from suppliers

25. Except as provided in the following rule, no Partner shall accept directly or indirectly any gift whatever or other reward from any individual or company or other group of individuals with whom or with which he has or is likely to have any dealings direct or indirect on the Partnership's behalf; nor shall he, without his Principal Director's written consent, make directly or indirectly any purchases whatever, except for the Partnership, from any source the acceptance of a gift from which would be a breach of the first part of this Rule.

26. A gift from a business connection of the Partnership may be accepted, when a Partner believes it to be offered as a harmless courtesy with no ill motive and when he hesitates to

refuse for fear of giving offence; the circumstances are most likely to arise in a foreign country and when the gift is in the form of hospitality.

27. If a gift so accepted is something other than hospitality and has money-value, the Partner shall pass it on to the appropriate council so that its value will accrue not to himself but to the Partnership. If the gift is hospitality, the Partner shall, if he thinks fit, return it either at the Partnership's expense or at his own.

28. A Partner shall report promptly and fully to his manager or Principal Director any attempt by an outsider to induce him to transgress the Partnership's Rules for its dealings with its suppliers. If in the judgment of the Partner receiving the report the matter was not a misunderstanding or trivial, he shall transmit the report promptly to the Chairman; and the Partnership, unless the Chairman direct in writing otherwise, shall take any legal proceedings possible under the Prevention of Corruption Acts or any other law for the prevention of corruption.

All Partners have access to these Rules. The John Lewis *Gazette* is a highly democratic journal that prints all readers' letters (most of which are anonymous) provided that they are not obscene, racially offensive or disclose confidential information about the Partnership. They are all answered by management. The examples below cover most of the issues relating to entertaining:

> Sir: During a recent dining-room conversation, I was told that some of the Management Services directors are being given tickets to major sporting events by some of our suppliers. Specifically, it was mentioned that one manager enjoys two days a year at Wimbledon at —'s expense, and another enjoys Premiership football, this time at —'s expense.
>
> Can we be informed as to whether this is true? I was under the impression that no Partner was to accept a gift from a supplier unless to refuse would cause extreme embarrassment. In this case, the gift should be donated to the Committee for Claims.
>
> Yours etc, 'All Partners Are Equal' (undated)

The Chief Registrar's comments began with an outline of the first three Rules as shown above. He then wrote:

> The Rules recognise that the offer of hospitality is more difficult to deal with, and say that it may be accepted if it is 'offered as a harmless courtesy with no ill motive and when [the Partner] hesitates to refuse for fear of giving offence'. They go on to say that the Partner may return the hospitality at either his own or the Partnership's expense.
>
> Several principles must be followed in considering whether such an offer of hospitality should be accepted; different directorates have their own arrangements for applying them. First and foremost, there must be clear benefit for the Partnership. Second, accepting the offer must not lead to the Partner having any sense of obligation to the supplier. Third, the hospitality accepted must be modest. Fourth, it must be capable of being repaid.

As for the specific point that this correspondent makes, the Director of Management Services tells me that such invitations are accepted only rarely in his directorate.

K D Temple

The next month another Partner decided to have a go at the people at the top:

Sir: With reference to recent correspondence concerning the acceptance of hospitality by senior Partners,... I should be very much surprised if such activities are confined to Management Services and suspect that other directors may well enjoy such privileges – the Chairman, obviously; the Finance Director, almost certainly; and possibly others such as the Directors of Buying.

We must, of course, accept that this is a part of business life and that attendance at sporting and other prestigious events may well result in the sort of networking that is ultimately beneficial to our business. Then again, it might not, and could turn out to be no more than a thoroughly enjoyable jolly for the director concerned, with no commercial benefit whatsoever.

Perhaps directors in receipt of such corporate hospitality should be expected to give a contribution of half-a-day's pay to the Central Committee for Claims and Retirement. I am sure that would accord with most Partners' views of fair play, especially those Partners on the shopfloor who may accept nothing from a grateful customer, or, if they do, have to pay for it – a perfectly acceptable and proper Partnership practice, but one where the same principle should be applied at all levels.

Yours etc 'Egalitarian' (6-9-96)

In the same issue another wrote challenging the way in which the management interpreted the Rules:

Sir: I read with concern the letter from All Partners Are Equal. I read the reply from Mr Temple with amazement. Could I deal in turn with each of the four principles which must be followed when deciding to accept an offer of hospitality.

1. There must be clear benefit to the Partnership. How does it benefit the Partnership for a manager to enjoy two days at Wimbledon, and another to enjoy Premiership football, at the expense of suppliers?

2. Accepting the offer must not lead to the Partner having any sense of obligation to the supplier. If that is the case, there is no requirement for the fourth principle, which I will mention later.

3. The hospitality accepted must be modest. Since a good seat at Wimbledon can cost several hundred pounds a day, and a season ticket for a senior football club about the same, I think Mr Temple should give us his opinion of the maximum amount of hospitality value that could be considered modest; what might appear modest to a senior director might give a more humble Partner severe palpitations.

4. [The hospitality] must be capable of being repaid. I see a nonsense here: if principle 2 is valid then principle 4 need not exist since there is no obligation to the supplier.

Mr Temple also makes the statement in his reply that the Partner receiving hospitality may return it at his own or the Partnership's expense. I wonder what proportion of Partners return hospitality at their own expense? I would like to know if the specific examples of hospitality referred to in the letter from All Partners Are Equal were returned and at whose expense. If, as I suspect, the answer is 'at the Partnership's expense' then I think Mr Temple should now state the cost that the Partnership has incurred in repaying this hospitality.

Mr Temple states that the invitations referred to in the original letter are accepted only rarely; I imagine once a year would be about right for the instances quoted.

Finally, can Mr Temple confirm that should a rank-and-file Partner like myself be fortunate enough to receive hospitality from a supplier – within the terms of his four principles, of course – then I would also be able to return this at the Partnership's expense?

Yours etc 'But Some More Than Others' (undated)

The Chief Registrar commented:

I can well understand the feelings that prompt these correspondents to write in these terms and to question why any senior Partnership manager should pick up 'treats'.

But as Egalitarian acknowledges, and as the Rules recognise, to accept hospitality is in certain circumstances of advantage to the Partnership. What I have said in my reply to All Partners Are Equal is that there are a limited number of occasions on which hospitality is accepted, that clear principles govern acceptance, and that the overriding consideration is that there must be clear benefit to the Partnership rather than to the individual Partner. The main safeguards against abuse in this area are personal integrity and self-discipline – which one hopes these correspondents observe as characteristic of Partnership managers – not the kind of arrangement Egalitarian advocates.

I am not surprised that But Some More than Others invites me to define tightly the circumstances in which hospitality might be accepted, but the four principles I set out in my earlier reply have to be expressed in general terms. Partners operate in widely different fields of activity; it really would make no sense to set down lengthy regulations to cover every eventuality. Those principles give a guide as to whether acceptance is in the Partnership's interest or not. (And, to the criticism of But Some More Than Others that the second and fourth principles are contradictory, I would say that one can wish to repay something without having an obligation to do so.)

K D Temple

The correspondence continued, but the above quotations are enough to show that it is very difficult to make rules to cover every eventuality and that the very existence of such rules can raise difficulties over highly controversial issues. The correspondence also reveals a great deal about the culture of John Lewis. The *Gazette* is a vehicle for Partners of any level to make their views known, whereas in other companies those views are probably felt but, on the whole, left unspoken.

Appendix E

Twelve steps for implementing a code of conduct

From Applying Codes of Business Ethics by Simon Webley (1995), published by the Institute of Business Ethics and reproduced with their permission.

1. **Integration** Produce a strategy for integrating the code into the running of the business at the time that it is issued.
2. **Endorsement** Make sure that the code is endorsed by the chairman and Chief Executive Officer.
3. **Distribution** Send the code to all employees in a readable and portable form and give it to all employees of the company.
4. **Breaches** Include a short section on how an employee can react if he or she is faced with a potential breach of the code or is in doubt about a course of action involving an ethical choice.
5. **Personal Response** Give all staff the personal opportunity to respond to the content of the code.
6. **Affirmation** Have a procedure for managers and supervisors regularly to state that they and their staff understand and apply the provisions of the code and raise matters not covered by it.
7. **Regular Review** Have a procedure for regular review and updating of the code.
8. **Contracts** Consider making adherence to the code obligatory by including reference to it in all contracts of employment and linking it with disciplinary procedures.
9. **Training** Ask those responsible for company training programmes at all

levels to include issues raised by the code in their programmes.

10. **Translation** See that the code is translated for use in overseas subsidiaries or other places where English is not the principal language.

11. **Distribution** Make copies of the code available to business partners (suppliers, customers etc).

12. **Annual Report** Reproduce or insert a copy of the code in the Annual Report so that shareholders and a wider public know about the company's position on ethical matters.

Appendix F

Shell's Statement of General Business Principles

Originally published in 1976, this statement has been revised from time to time, the version below being that published in 1997. It is reproduced with the permission of Shell International Limited, to whom any requests for further copies should be addressed.

INTRODUCTION

This document reaffirms the general business principles that govern how each of the Shell companies which make up the Royal Dutch Shell Group of Companies conducts its affairs.

The Group is a decentralized, diversified group of companies with widespread activities, and each Shell company has wide freedom of action. However what we have in common is the Shell reputation. Upholding the Shell reputation is paramount. We are judged by how we act. Our reputation will be upheld if we act with honesty and integrity in all our dealings and we do what we think is right at all times within the legitimate role of business.

Shell companies have as their core values honesty, integrity and respect for people. Shell companies also firmly believe in the fundamental importance of the promotion of trust, openness, teamwork and professionalism, and in pride in what they do.

Our underlying corporate values determine our principles. These principles apply to all transactions, large or small, and describe the behaviour expected of every employee in every Shell company in the conduct of its business.

In turn, the application of these principles is underpinned by procedures within each Shell company which are designed to make sure that its employees understand the principles and that they act in accordance with them. We recognize that it is vital that our behaviour matches our intentions.

All the elements of this structure – values, principles and the accompanying procedures – are necessary.

Shell companies recognize that maintaining the trust and confidence of shareholders, employees, customers and other people with whom they do business, as well as the communities in which they work, is crucial to the Group's continued growth and success.

We intend to merit this trust by conducting ourselves according to the standards set out in our principles. These principles have served Shell companies well for many years. It is the responsibility of management to ensure that all employees are aware of these principles, and behave in accordance with the spirit as well as the letter of this statement.

C A J Herkströter
Chairman of the Committee of Managing Directors
March 1997

1. OBJECTIVES

The objectives of Shell companies are to engage efficiently, responsibly and profitably in the oil, gas, chemicals and other selected businesses and to participate in the search for and development of other sources of energy. Shell companies seek a high standard of performance and aim to maintain a long-term position in their respective competitive environments.

2. RESPONSIBILITIES

Shell companies recognize five areas of responsibility:

a. To shareholders
To protect shareholders' investment, and provide an acceptable return.

b. To customers
To win and maintain customers by developing and providing products and services which offer value in terms of price, quality, safety and environmental impact, which are supported by the requisite technological, environmental and commercial expertise.

c. To employees

To respect the human rights of their employees, to provide their employees with good and safe conditions of work, and good and competitive terms and conditions of service, to promote the development and best use of human talent and equal opportunity employment, and to encourage the involvement of employees in the planning and direction of their work, and in the application of these principles within their company. It is recognized that commercial success depends on the full commitment of all employees.

d. To those with whom they do business

To seek mutually beneficial relationships with contractors, suppliers and in joint ventures and to promote the application of these principles in so doing. The ability to promote these principles effectively will be an important factor in the decision to enter into or remain in such relationships.

e. To society

To conduct business as responsible corporate members of society, to observe the laws of the countries in which they operate, to express support for fundamental human rights in line with the legitimate role of business and to give proper regard to health, safety and the environment consistent with their commitment to contribute to sustainable development.

These five areas of responsibility are seen as inseparable. Therefore it is the duty of management continuously to assess the priorities and discharge its responsibilities as best it can on the basis of that assessment.

3. ECONOMIC PRINCIPLES

Profitability is essential to discharging these responsibilities and staying in business. It is a measure both of efficiency and of the value that customers place on Shell products and services. It is essential to the allocation of the necessary corporate resources and to support the continuing investment required to develop and produce future energy supplies to meet consumer needs. Without profits and a strong financial foundation it would not be possible to fulfil the responsibilities outlined above.

Shell companies work in a wide variety of changing social, political and economic environments, but in general they believe that the interests of the community can be served most efficiently by a market economy.

Criteria for investment decisions are not exclusively economic in nature but also take into account social and environmental considerations and an appraisal of the security of the investment.

4. BUSINESS INTEGRITY

Shell companies insist on honesty, integrity and fairness in all aspects of their business and expect the same in their relationships with all those with whom they do business. The direct or indirect offer, payment, soliciting and acceptance of bribes in any form are unacceptable practices.

Employees must avoid conflicts of interest between their private financial activities and their part in the conduct of company business. All business transactions on behalf of a Shell company must be reflected accurately and fairly in the accounts of the company in accordance with established procedures and be subject to audit.

5. POLITICAL ACTIVITIES

a. Of companies

Shell companies act in a socially responsible manner within the laws of the countries in which they operate in pursuit of their legitimate commercial objectives. Shell companies do not make payments to political parties, organizations or their representatives or take any part in party politics. However, when dealing with governments, Shell companies have the right and the responsibility to make their position known on any matter which affects themselves, their employees, their customers, or their shareholders. They also have the right to make their position known on matters affecting the community, where they have a contribution to make.

b. Of employees

Where individuals wish to engage in activities in the community, including standing for election to public office, they will be given the opportunity to do so where this is appropriate in the light of local circumstances.

6. HEALTH, SAFETY AND THE ENVIRONMENT

Consistent with their commitment to contribute to sustainable development, Shell companies have a systematic approach to health, safety and environmental management in order to achieve continuous performance improvement.

To this end Shell companies manage these matters as any other critical business activity, set targets for improvement, and measure, appraise and report performance.

7. THE COMMUNITY

The most important contribution that companies can make to the social and material progress of the countries in which they operate is in performing their basic activities as effectively as possible. In addition Shell companies take a constructive interest in societal matters which may not be directly related to the business. Opportunities for involvement - for example through community, educational or donations programmes - will vary depending upon the size of the company concerned, the nature of the local society, and the scope for useful private initiatives.

8. COMPETITION

Shell companies support free enterprise. They seek to compete fairly and ethically and within the framework of applicable competition laws; they will not prevent others from competing freely with them.

9. COMMUNICATION

Shell companies recognize that in view of the importance of the activities in which they are engaged and their impact on national economies and individuals, open communication is essential. To this end, Shell companies have comprehensive corporate information programmes and provide full relevant information about their activities to legitimately interested parties, subject to any overriding considerations of business confidentiality and cost.

Appendix G

List of some relevant organizations

The Accounting Standards Board
Holborn Hall, 100 Gray's Inn Road, London WC1X 8AL
Tel: 0171 404 8818 Fax: 0171 404 4497
E-mail: mailbox@frc-asb.demon.co.uk

The role of the ASB is to make, amend and withdraw accounting standards. It took over this role from the Accounting Standards Committee in 1990. Unlike the latter, it is autonomous; it does not need outside approval for its actions, but it does consult widely on all its proposals. Its general aim in the making of accounting standards is to centre them as far as possible on principles rather than highly prescriptive rules.

The Advertising Association
15 Wilton Road, London SW1V 1NJ
Tel: 0171 828 2771 Fax: 0171 931 0376
E-mail: aa@adassac.org.uk

The Advertising Association is a federation of trade associations and professional bodies representing advertisers, agencies, the media and support services. It promotes and protects freedom to advertise in conformity with established codes of practice.

Business in the Community (BitC)
44 Baker Street, London W1M 1DH
Tel: 0171 224 1600 Fax: 0171 486 1700
E-mail: information@BitC.org.uk

Founded in 1982, BitC is an association of some 400 companies which use their skills, expertise, influence, products and profits to promote regeneration in partnership with each other, the public and the voluntary and educational sectors. It is a registered charity supported by the contribution of member companies.

Centre for Tomorrow's Company
19 Buckingham Street, London WC2N 6EF
Tel: 0171 930 5150 Fax: 0171 930 5155
E-mail: ctomco@ctomco.demon.co.uk

The Centre, which originated from the RSA's Inquiry into Tomorrow's Company, is a catalyst and think-tank created in 1996 to inspire and enable UK businesses to increase their profits by including their people, customers, suppliers and communities as well as their shareholders as primary relationships. Its Forum at the RSA brings together business leaders, investors, policy-makers and educators in debates and seminars to concentrate key minds on the issues that matter most for the future performance of organizations.

The Chartered Institute of Marketing (CIM)
Moor Hall, Cookham, Maidenhead, Berkshire SL6 9QH
Tel: 01628 427500 Fax: 01628 427499
E-mail: marketing@cim.co.uk

The CIM is a professional body with 60,000 members. One of the organization's objectives is to promote and maintain, for the benefit of the public, high standards of professional skill, ability and integrity among persons engaged in marketing products and services. It is a condition of membership to adhere to its Code of Professional Standards.

Chemical Industries Association Ltd
Kings Buildings, Smith Square, London SW1P 3JJ
Tel: 0171 834 3399 Fax: 0171 834 4469
E-mail: enquiries@cia.org.uk

The Chemical Industries Association is the main representative organization for the UK chemical industry, being both a trade and employers' association with some 200 members. Along with leading member companies it is affiliated to CEFIC, the European Chemical Industries Federation. It promotes the Responsible Care initiative for continuous improvement in health, safety and environmental performance.

Confederation of British Industry (CBI)
Centre Point, 103 New Oxford Street, London WC1A 1DU
Tel: 0171 379 7400 Fax: 0171 497 2597
E-mail: information.centre@cbi.org.uk

The CBI is Britain's business voice, representing more than 250,000 public and private companies, and lobbies the UK government and the EU Commission. It is consulted widely by many governments, civil servants and the media on business issues. It offers members research services, advice and publications.

The Environment Council
21 Elizabeth Street, London SW1W 9RP
Tel: 0171 824 8411 Fax: 0171 730 9941
E-mail: environment.council@ukonline.co.uk

Established in 1970, the Environment Council is an independent charity dedicated to protecting the UK's environment by promoting effective dialogue between organizations with potentially conflicting views, namely government, business, the environmental sector and the community, to find environmental solutions that work. Since 1988, it has established practical partnerships with companies and individuals, working with them to address the environmental issues they face and to develop appropriate strategies.

HUB Initiative
Institute of Directors, 116 Pall Mall, London SW1Y 5ED
Tel: 0171 451 3377 Fax: 0171 925 2310
E-mail: HUB@iod.org.uk

So-called because business is at the heart of all our lives, HUB aims to promote the highest standards of behaviour by business and business people and a more positive view of the vital contribution that business makes. Through HUB's ambassador programme, business people speak up for business in dialogue with the public.

Institute of Business Ethics (IBE)
12 Palace Street, London SW1E 5JA
Tel: 0171 931 0495 Fax: 0171 821 5819
E-mail: info@ibe.org.uk

The IBE was founded in 1986. It seeks to clarify ethical issues in business, to propose positive solutions to problems and to establish common ground with people of goodwill of all faiths. It is business based, has a positive approach to wealth creation and deals with current ethical issues in a practical manner. It endeavours to identify best practice in business to make it more widely known. It publishes papers and books on the subject, several of which are listed in the bibliography.

Institute of Directors (IoD)

116 Pall Mall, London SW1Y 5ED
Tel: 0171 839 1233 Fax: 0171 925 2310
E-mail: businessinfo@iod.co.uk

Founded in 1903, the IoD is a club for individual members that aims to be the prime organization helping directors fulfil their leadership responsibilities in creating wealth for the benefit of business and society as a whole. It has published the *Director* magazine since 1947 and has numerous publications relevant to members.

Institute for Global Ethics

PO Box 563, Camden, Maine 04843, USA
Tel: 207 236 6658 Fax: 207 236 4014
E-mail: ige@world.std.com
London office:
16 Northwick Close
London NW8 8DG
Tel: 0171 266 5404 Fax: 0171 266 0404
E-mail: northwick@easynet.co.uk

A membership-based, non-profit body that aims to: discover and articulate the global common ground of ethical values; analyse ethical trends and shifts in values as they develop round the world; gather and disseminate information on global ethics; and elevate public awareness and discussion of the issues.

Institute of Management

2 Savoy Court, Strand, London WC2R 0EZ
Tel: 0171 497 0580 Fax: 0171 497 0463
E-mail: savoy@inst-mgt.org.uk

The Institute of Management is a membership organization the mission of which is to promote the art and science of management through research, education and training.

International Business Ethics Institute

Suite 503, 1000 Connecticut Avenue NW, Washington DC 20036, USA
Tel: 202 296 6938 Fax: 202 296 5897

The Institute offers professional services to organizations interested in implementing, expanding or modifying business ethics and corporate responsibility programmes. Its unique approach combines the compliance-orientation of traditional ethics programmes with broader examinations of corporate integrity and company values.

International Chamber of Commerce (ICC)
38 Cours Albert 1er, 75008 Paris, France
Tel: (1) 49 53 28 59 Fax: (1) 49 53 28 59
E-mail: icc@iccwbo.org

Founded in 1919, the ICC is the world's leading business representative organization with members in over 130 countries. It is a non-profit, non-governmental
body which stands for liberalized trade based on fair competition, and promotes
self-regulation within a framework of law. It represents business to
inter-governmental organizations and governments on all the key issues that affect business internationally and has developed codes of conduct on advertising, marketing, bribery and the environment.

ICC United Kingdom
14–15 Belgrave Square, London SW1X 8PS
Tel: 0171 823 2811 Fax: 0171 235 5447
E-mail: 106142. 2273@compuserve.com

Founded in 1919, ICC United Kingdom is the British affiliate of the ICC,
through which British members influence and participate in the work of the ICC
internationally. It also represents ICC views to the UK Government.

Investors in People
7–10 Chandos Street, London W1M 9DE
Tel: 0171 467 1900 Fax: 0171 636 2386
E-mail: investors-in-people-uk@dial.pipex.com

Investors in People is the national quality-standard setter for effective investment in the training and development of all people. As a standard and a bench-
mark, it aims to improve UK business effectiveness and performance by
encouraging employers to develop the skills of their people to achieve business
goals.

The Portman Group
2d Wimpole Street, London W1M 7AA
Tel: 0171 499 1010 Fax: 0171 493 1417

The Portman Group was founded by the major UK drinks producers to promote
sensible drinking and reduce alcohol abuse. The companies represent a high
proportion of UK alcoholic drinks production and substantial retail capacity.
Since its inception in 1989, the Group's advocacy of sensible drinking has been
responsive to public concerns to ensure that alcohol is enjoyed by adult consumers only, and its Code of Practice on the naming, packaging and merchan-
dising of alcoholic drinks was produced for this purpose.

Royal Society of Arts
8 John Adam Street, London WC2N 6EZ
Tel: 0171 930 5115 Fax: 0171 839 5805
E-mail: rsa@rsa.ftech.co.uk

Founded in 1754, the Royal Society for the Encouragement of Arts, Manufactures and Commerce (its full name) has some 20,000 Fellows of accomplishment from every walk of life (some thirteen per cent of whom come from outside the UK). It is an instrument of change that works to create a civilized society based on a sustainable economy. It uses its independence and the resources of its Fellowship in the UK and overseas to stimulate discussion, develop ideas and encourage action. Particularly relevant to this book are its projects on *Tomorrow's Company* and *Ethics in the Workplace*.

Transparency International
Heylstrasse 33, D-10825 Berlin, Germany
Tel: (49) 30 787 59 08 Fax: (49) 30 787 57 07
E-mail: ti@contrib.de

Transparency International is a non-profit making, non-governmental organization, working to counter corruption both in international business transactions and at national level, through national chapters. It encourages governments to establish and implement effective laws against corruption, seeks to influence through its Standards of Conduct all parties in business transactions to operate at the highest level of integrity and strengthens public support for these objectives.

Index